KARMIC ASTROLOGY

KARMIC ASTROLOGY

♈ ♉ ♊ ♋ ♌ ♍ ♎ ♏ ♐ ♑ ♒ ♓

RETROGRADES AND REINCARNATION

Volume II
In A Series By

MARTIN SCHULMAN

SAMUEL WEISER, INC.

York Beach, Maine

First published in 1977 by
Samuel Weiser, Inc.
Box 612
York Beach, Maine 03910-0612

99 98 97 96
18 17 16 15 14

Library of Congress Catalog Card Number: 83-104490

ISBN 0-87728-345-1
MG

Printed in the United States of America

The paper used in this publication meets the minimum require-
ments of the American National Standard for Permanence of Paper
for Printed Library Materials Z39.48-1984.

. . . . .*To my Dearest little Princess Penny Sue*

Who like a flower grows and blossoms
Amidst the thorns and weeds.
And from gentle drops of rain
That moisten her thirsty petals,
She blooms endlessly. . . . .

Author's Note

More often than not, planets appear in retrograde motion when they are in opposition to the sun. Thus, they often symbolize a vortex in consciousness which might be called the *not-Sun* of reality. The reader is cautioned not to attempt to experience the retrograde vibration on intuitive or psychic levels because the effect of so many retrograde placements can easily put an individual out of harmony with his own vibration. It is therefore suggested that, except for those particular planetary placements which appear in your own chart, this book should be read with enough impersonal detachment so that you are not pulled into the full vortex of the retrograde vibration.

TABLE OF CONTENTS

Editor's Note

Because the author felt a strong need to produce a more contemporary work, the following planetary placements have been omitted:

1. Uranus in Capricorn through Pisces
2. Neptune in Aries through Cancer, and Capricorn through Pisces
3. Pluto in Aries through Gemini, and Sagittarius through Pisces.

Most of these are either too far into the future or, in many but not all cases, far enough in the past to limit current interest.

If it becomes necessary to study any of these placements, one may read a corresponding House position relating to the planet in question, i.e. for Uranus in Pisces, read Uranus in the Twelfth House. Here it is important to keep the element of the sign, its ruler and its quality in mind so that one may be guided to a practical interpretation. Planetary Phases may be similarly deduced, but with less exactitude. Here, as with all astrological interpretation, close observation, awareness of the entire natal chart, and a knowledge of the person's life history will give one the information necessary for a reasonable interpretation.

Clark Stillman

INTRODUCTION

Students and Astrologers alike go to much trouble to be sure to notate whether or not a planet is Retrograde when drawing up a chart. But, what happens after that? Aside from a rather vague understanding that such a planet may not be giving the individual the benefits he derives from direct motion planets, any attempts to interpret the exact meanings of these obvious "oddities" have been not only confusing but lacking in any agreeable understanding throughout the field. As a result, the entire subject carries with it a rather mysterious intrigue clouded by numerous guesses which seem to contradict each other.

The problem for the most part has been the multiple dimensions of the Retrograde effect. We know that in many areas of Astrology, the proper interpretation lies in discovering the dimension through which a particular planet, sign, house, or aspect is working for the individual. The same is true of Retrograde planets. While Astrologers have been looking for the "one" true obvious effect, they have missed the very obvious fact that Retrogrades work in different ways at the same time. This is probably the main reason why the entire subject has not been clearly understood before now.

Retrograde planets open up a new and much deeper understanding of an individual than Astrology has heretofore attempted to discover. They are in fact, a rather unique experience in consciousness; describing so much of what actually happens within an individual whether or not it finds expression in his outer life. And, the fascinating part of all of this is the tremendous amount of thoughtfulness, introspection and depth that a person can achieve through understanding and using his Retrograde planets.

After much study on this subject it becomes easy to see how things in life can be different from each other without one necessarily being better or worse than another.

The author hopes that these pages will help those who seek to understand the Retrograde Process.

PART ONE

RETROGRADES

AN EXPERIENCE IN RELATIVITY

RETROGRADES AND MAGNETISM

There is nothing in the universe that doesn't have magnetic qualities. Thought itself is known to attract similar thought.

Each individual has his own magnetic energies based entirely upon how the makeup of his planetary horoscope arrangement is used. All configurations attract certain things and at the same time repel others. Thus, the whole world is in a positive and negative condition at the same time.

In the individual horoscope some planets are positioned in a point of radiation where they constantly give out their energies to the world. Others are positioned as points of absorption through which the individual is able to assimilate the understanding he needs of the universe.

Truly, it is how the individual uses his planets which will determine their magnetic qualities at any particular moment above and beyond the basic magnetic quality of the planet. Thus, even planets which absorb can radiate, depending upon how the individual himself is polarized at any particular moment.

When a person is experiencing a great deal of energy, beyond what he needs at the time, most of his planets acts as radiators and he becomes a giver to others. In the opposite condition, when a person is experiencing less energy than he needs to function, his planets become absorbers, drawing from others the energy he is lacking.

Man has the ability from moment to moment to actually control his own magnetic field! To see this, consider the planet Venus, which itself is negatively magnetized and is generally thought of as an absorber. Yet, when an individual has, through all his other planets, more energy than he needs at any given moment, he will use his Venus to radiate love to others. The same applies to Mars, often thought of as aggressively masculine and self-centered. In the same circumstances, when an individual has more energy than he needs, he uses his Mars to energize others. This occurs with all the planets. From moment to moment and day to day, each planet is in part a radiator and in part an absorber.

It is to what extent one holds dominance over the other at any given point in an individual's life that Astrology concerns itself. And the Astrologer tries to the best of his ability, to teach individuals how to use their planets in both ways.

When an individual is able to use all of his planets as radiators and absorbers, switching their polarity as is needed, he does not need a horoscope reading. But, there is rarely an Astrology reading in which this is so. Usually, the individual is either absorbing or radiating too much or too little in terms of how he combines and blends all the planetary energies in his chart. To the layman, this is defined as having personal problems that one does not know how to cope with. To the Astrologer it is only a polarization of magnetic energy and, as soon as the individual can be brought to understand and to develop control over his own magnetic force fields, much of his personal problems miraculously disappear!

There is no question that Retrograde planets create quite a different force field for the individual to deal with than planets in direct motion. It has been the general lack of understanding of this force field that has caused so many individuals to expereince so many personal difficulties in this area.

The general tendency is for the individual to try to use his Retrogrades in exactly the same manner as he is using his planets which are in direct motion. And when this doesn't work he starts dividing himself into various unrelated states which can result in general misery.

With planets in direct motion it is very easy for the individual to switch the emphasis of the planetary energy within himself from moment to moment as his own total energy pattern rises and falls. However, when he tries to do this with his Retrograde planets he runs into quite a different situation.

Firstly, he is at any given time going through part of a threefold Retrograde Process. He is:

1. Jumping ahead of himself trying to live the future now,

2. In the process of living out the future, experiencing the feelings that he has already been there,

3. Repeating in mind the first phase, so that he is actually reliving the looking forward to a future that has already occurred.

When the individual is in Phase I (jumping ahead of himself into trying to live the future now) it is nearly impossible for him to employ the Retrograde planet negatively, for he is trying to use all his energy for the propulsion of forward motion. Thus, during this Phase he radiates outward so that he can magnetize himself towards all people and conditions which will bring about the future experience.

During Phase II (when he is actually living out the experience) he is often unaware of Phase I where he actually brought it about. But he does experience more deja-vu feelings than direct motion planet individuals. In other words he has the sense to know that he has experienced this before, but he doesn't know exactly how, when or why. It is this ambivalence that creates a cross vibration where he is operating negatively and positively at the same time. Part of him is positively radiating his desire to complete the experience, while the other part of him is negatively seeking to absorb the understanding of why the experience feels repetitive to him. Naturally, it is during this phase that the individual is least understood by others.

Finally in Phase III where he is repeating in mind the looking forward to a future that he has already lived through, he becomes completely out of time synchronization with the rest of the world as he attempts to reabsorb the individuals and circumstances which will bring him back to his past. He is more understandable during this phase, but he is also more of an energy drain on others because he is radiating practically no outward energy.

It is interesting to note that Phases I and II — the attempt to live in the future and the cross-vibration of future-past, are so private to the individual that Astrology hardly notices these as characteristic of the Retrograde. Instead, it has always been Phase III of the Retrograde Process (the past lingering or repeating characteristic) that has always been the most noticeable. Perhaps this is because this final phase is where the individual not only spends most of his time but also reacts in a more observably different way than society at large.

RETROGRADES AND THE TIME FACTOR

Because of the threefold Retrograde Process, the individual experiences his life in different time sequences than those individuals with direct-motion planets. In fact, the parts of his life influenced by Retrogrades are quite different than the parts of his life that he experiences through his own direct-motion planets.

When the sequence of events in his mind is running in contrary motion or changing direction away from the sequence of events in his life, he is actually breaking the time barrier. Depending upon which phase he is in, he is living at least part of his life in a different type of time warp. Here in this amazing transcendence of time through Retrogrades is the major key to Karma.

RETROGRADES AND KARMA

Not only do Retrogrades cause the individual to regress back to yesterday, last month and last year, but they also induce regression back to former lives whose memories carry strongly into the present incarnation. These memories represent specific events or individuals that were meaningful enough in another life to still have a hold on the person now.

Wherever a Retrograde planet appears in the horoscope, the individual does not come forward in time sequence along with the rest of his chart. Instead, he keeps trying to resolve the earlier circumstances which still appear to be unfinished.

In these specific areas of his life there does not seem to be a demarcation between one life and another. His memories are so vivid that he doesn't even recognize them as memories. But rather they seem to him to be the present. Nevertheless he is living in a dulled phase of another time zone whose irresistible magnetism seems even more important than his current life.

RETROGRADES APPEARING IN SIGNS

A Retrograde planet appearing in a sign takes on the entire coloring of that sign and directs its energies backward in time. The individual relives in this life the exact same kind of experiences he has already been through in past incarnations in relation to the specific Retrograde planet. But, for some reason, perhaps inner soul feelings that the Karmic lesson was unfinished, or not worked out to the personal satisfaction of the lower self, the individual keeps bringing those same situations forward into this life. The truth is, he is trying to bring this life back to the unsolved one. And, since the quality of life as well as one's place in it is based on one's perception of the world around him, this individual is not really living in the present time zone with respect to his Retrograde planets.

For this reason, Astrologers have always felt that Retrograde planets do not work to their best potential. It is not that they don't work well as much as the fact that the individual is not applying them that much to his current life. Instead he is trying to make the world today fit into his past concepts. Obviously, it is this type of living that causes a great part of the disharmony that is so often ascribed to Retrograde planets.

The threefold Retrograde Process, which acts not only in this lifetime but also has a tendency to break through time barriers into other lifetimes, acts slightly differently in each sign. For example, the individual with Mercury Retrograde in Aries, experiencing Phase I (leaping in time ahead of himself) would be presenting himself positively, which is completely harmonious with the Martian quality of the sign. During Phase III (where he is moving backwards in his thought processes) he would be totally out of harmony with the Aries vibration. Perhaps this is the reason why people with Mercury Retrograde in Aries experience so much tension in their lives and rarely feel united with their thoughts and the ability to act them out.

The individual with Retrograde Mercury in Taurus is least in harmony with himself during Phase I. The leaping ahead in time of the Retrograde totally contradicts the receptive dormant qualities of the Venus-ruled Earth sign which would be more at home in the security experienced during Phase II in which the individual can live out his energy patterns along a path he vaguely senses is familiar.

Thus, with each Retrograde planet the individual is more in tune with himself during one or another phase of the threefold Retrograde Process depending very strongly upon the nature of the sign the Retrograde is found in.

Astrology, up to now, has dealt more with the effects of Retrogrades than their actual process but it is by the understanding of this process that the individual can at least know when he is in tune or out of tune and why!

The actual triggering of the process starts the moment the individual experiences his first thought directed toward any desired goal of expression. The length of each phase depends very much upon the sign the planet is posited in. Man always tries to prolong his experiences of pleasure and shorten his experiences of pain. Thus, whichever phase of the Retrograde Process is most in harmony with the sign the Retrograde is in, can be expected to be displayed longer in time, and therefore outwardly be seen as more characteristic of the individual. At the same time, whichever phase is most out of harmony with the characteristics of the sign is not only displayed less in time but also reflects many of the individual's complaints about his life.

RETROGRADES APPEARING IN HOUSES

When a Retrograde appears in a house it focuses the threefold Retrograde Process into that area of experience that the house represents. The individual will seek to expand in time that phase of the Retrograde Process that is most in harmony with the house through which he will express it and he will try to decrease in time that phase which is least in harmony with the house areas of experience.

Consider an individual with Venus Retrograde in the Tenth house. The planet is most harmonious with the house experience during Phase III where it is possible to repeat in mind that which has already been experienced. This is because the Tenth house symbolizes achievement crystallized, not the working towards it as much as the fulfillment from it. Thus, when the individual is able to magnetically absorb the appreciation of his peers for work well done he is most in harmony with his Tenth house Retrograde Venus. And, as a result, this will be seen as the more characteristic meaning of this planetary placement for him, as he seeks to expand this phase of absorption in time.

The most negative expression of his Tenth house Venus Retrograde will be found when he is going through the Retrograde Phase I (the leaping ahead in time), which is so uncharacteristic of Venus but also totally disharmonious with the restrictive Saturn ruled Tenth house, he can be found complaining of how much effort he sees in front of him. As a result, during Phase I, where he is manifesting his Venus positively towards a constructive future, all he can see is the seemingly insurmountable walls of Saturnian experiences before him. Perhaps this is why he desires so much appreciation by the time he actually completes it through to Phase III. In this particular planetary placement, the individual experiences positive feelings during Phase II where he is traversing on safe ground towards a specific goal.

As another example, consider the individual with Mars Retrograde in the Twelfth house. During Phase I, Mars is in harmony with itself as it strives to leap into the future, but at the same time is totally out of harmony with the house experience which is deeply rooted in the past. During Phase III, where the Retrograde is naturally reviewing past experiences, Mars is in complete harmony with the past tendencies of the house, but totally out of harmony with the futuristic qualities of Mars itself. During Phase II, where the individual is living out that which he has already had prior glimpses of, the Mars quality of desire for action is fulfilled at the same time that its Retrograde (or backward nature) is agreeing with the qualities of the Twelfth house (of the past). Thus, it is Phase II which is the most comfortable for this individual and as a result, it is this phase that he tries to live in most of the time. Consequently, he is seen by others as repeating in action most of his past-life Karma. And, whether society likes him to do this or not, it is by far the most comfortable way for him to live. When he tries to live in Phase I, he is pulled back by the experiences of the Twelfth house which make him too uncomfortable about his present actions. At the same time when he tries to live in Phase III, he finds it too difficult to magnetically absorb vibrations through the actively expressive Mars. But it is during the second phase, where he is caught in a cross-vibration of opposing forces that he is, believe it or not, the most at home with the true nature of his entire being.

RETROGRADES AND INDIVIDUALITY

It is interesting to see how the signs and houses in which Retrogrades appear will lead an individual to select which phase of the Retrograde Process he is most comfortable living in. As a result different individuals having the same planets Retrograde, but falling in different signs or houses will naturally display different phases of the Retrograde Process. Therefore, individuals with the same planets Retrograde can act differently.

It is for this reason that the true nature of Retrogrades has been so illusive for so many years; for inherent in it lies an immeasurably large number of choices through which original individual expression can be achieved. Quite literally, the combination of twelve possible houses with 360 degrees for the same sign Retrograde planet leaves us with one very distinct possibility. And that is, that approximately one out of every four thousand three hundred and twenty individuals is likely to use a Retrograde planet in exactly the same way as another individual. Naturally, this makes the job of interpretation on the part of the Astrologer quite difficult as well as explaining more graphically why for so many years Retrogrades remained in the domain of the unknown. But, in a more realistic sense it points out again the amount of freedom an individual maintains in making the personal life choices of how to use his planets.

RETROGRADES AND
MULTIPLE DIMENSIONS

In order to understand the full nature of Retrogrades, it is important to realize that they are operating through multiple dimensions at the same time. First, the individual experiences the threefold Retrograde Process, which has a strong tendency to throw him out of synchronization with the present moment. But, at the same time that he is going through any one of the phases of this process, he is also trying to correct Karma from another lifetime. Thus, he is either behind or ahead of himself in this life while still another part of himself is not yet in this life at all.

In addition to this lack of synchronization with chronological time, which in itself would be enough to upset most individuals, he also experiences on still another plane, a rather unique orientation in space.

RETROGRADES AND
THE SPACE FACTOR

A person in Phase I of the Retrograde Process (leaping ahead of himself to try to make the future occur now) is trying to present himself so magnetically positive that he is actually moving much closer in space to objects and people than the individual without Retrogrades. It is during this phase that he infringes on the auras of others, chops off the ends of people's sentences and literally begs, borrows or steals all substance in form that he feels is necessary to his experience. All people have a psychic space around them which is personally private to the point that predictable annoyance is demonstrated whenever this space is violated by others. To prove this, the next time you are in a restaurant with another individual, try in your most subtle manner to slide a piece of silverware over the imaginary centerline of the table, and watch the reaction of the individual you are dining with as he or she feels you invading the psychic space which is not yours. This is very much what happens with an individual as he experiences Phase I of the Retrograde Process. In as many ways as he possibly can, he is expanding his own psychic space.

It is during this period that he appears to be offensively aggressive to those around him. In Phase II where he is living out in action all the information and space he has already mapped out for himself, he experiences much less of a problem in getting along with others, but the moment he moves into Phase III, where he is looking back with expectancy towards a future that has already passed, he becomes highly introverted. As he draws into himself, he uses less and less space during this period and can't understand why others use so much. It is during this time that the individual actually pulls away from others, and here we have what has been for so many years classified as the Retrograde's most noticable behavior characteristic. Still, while he is regressing into his past, he is also absorbing the radiations of everything around him. And, although he objects to this absorption, he needs it in order to give birth to the moment when he will enter a new Phase I experience where he will again begin to radiate energy and expand time and space.

RETROGRADES AND THE LAW OF RELATIVITY

Because the Retrograde's different conceptions of time leads an individual to also experience changing perceptions in space, the ultimate life experience is always uniquely different than what one would call the norm. According to the laws of relativity, nothing in the universe exists alone, but rather operates in accordance with the laws of everything else it is connected to. Thus, the wheels of a car move in direct proportion to the accelerator pedal pressure. At the same time, the ground itself seems to move in relation to the wheels, and so on throughout the universe. Just as direct-motion planet individuals have their perception of time and space and through this perception live their lives, so does the Retrograde individual* have his time and space relationships. But, his perception of these planes of existence is different than that of the individual without Retrograde planets. In fact, his orientation in time and space through

*Retrograde Individual: This term used often throughout the book refers to an individual having three or more Retrogrades in his chart, any one of the inner planets Retrograde, or even one single Retrograde positioned near the Ascendant or Midheaven.

Retrogrades is also different than the time and space orientation he experiences in other parts of himself through his direct-motion planets. One part of him is relative to the universe in one way while other parts of him are relative to the universe in still other ways. It is important to see that the universe acts on him in great measure according to the ways in which he relatively perceives it.

Some people perceive the entire world through the eyes of matter, substance and form. Others see the world through the window of Spirit. And still a few others experience their relationship with the world around them through the vision of their Soul. Most people experience a blending of all of these, with one or another taking precedence at any one time over the others. The Retrograde planet, with its powerful Karmic lessons being brought forward in this life tends to emphasize the matter or form side of life, throwing man into the more primitive parts of himself where his struggle for survival amidst the conditions and people around him becomes predominant over the fulfillment of his Soul. This becomes even more heightened in the case of the inner Retrogrades (Mercury, Venus and Mars) through which man deals with the very same intimate, personal, and private parts of himself which he has been struggling with since his beginning in time. And while it is undoubtedly true that as man moves from one phase of the Retrograde Process into another tending to slightly shift his emphasis between matter-spirit-and soul, it should be remembered that soul and spirit are above the laws of Karma. Thus, there is always a residual hint of substance and matter (particularly etheric) throughout the Retrograde Phases.

These traces of etheric or astral matter which nearly always accompany the expression of Retrogrades carry the information for Karmic fulfillment. And, because matter is involved, one always feels another individual's Retrograde planets as being slightly or sometimes unusually heavier than direct-motion planets. It is because of this fact, that individuals who express themselves through their Retrogrades have a tremendous ability to make strong impressions on their listeners. The person they are talking to may choose to momentarily ignore the words, but it is difficult to ignore the etheric or astral matter which has been sent along with the words, and which will keep the message embedded in the individual's memory until he is either ready to accept or discard it based on future information he will add to it. For this reason, the thought forms of a Retrograde individual are unusually strong, and particularly during Phase I (where they are expanded and put out with some amount of force) become particularly difficult to walk away from even though the natural tendency because of the way they are expressed is to do exactly that!

RETROGRADES AND EVOLUTION

Not all people have Retrograde planets, but more people do than one might expect. Studies have shown that approximately 92 percent of the world's population has at least one Retrograde planet, and that it is not at all uncommon to have up to three Retrogrades. Since these planets have the ability to bring the past forward and the "forward" back into the past, it easy to see how they represent on a cosmic level, mankind's thread of continuity between the present and the past evolution of the entire race.

RETROGRADES AND SEXUALITY

Retrogrades are one of the primary causes of sexual difficulties in the world today. Sexual richness and fulfillment is based almost entirely on the consciousness of two individuals meeting and blending on all levels of time and space.

The individual with a Retrograde influencing his sexuality is unable to experience this total harmony. Since he is always in one Retrograde phase or another, his time and space perceptions do much to hinder him from fully experiencing the here and now.

Males with Venus Retrograde tend to be (at the very innermost parts of their being) more content in avoiding females. At the same time, females with Mars Retrograde experience similar difficulties in relating to males. When Mercury or Uranus appears Retrograde, sexuality is disturbed by an over-activity of the threefold Retrograde Process on the mental plane. In such cases the individual be-

comes too mentally activated to experience a balanced richness of sexuality in its physical and emotional context.

When Pluto is Retrograde, all current life sexuality is
based upon past-life sexual memories buried deep in the
unconscious. Thus while an individual is living in the present, his sexual nature can reflect the preferences and morality that he became accustomed to during an earlier and
generally less-evolved period in world history.

It is important to understand here that normal
heterosexuality starts out in a highly polarized magnetic
state of opposite energies moving towards neutrality in its
completion. Homosexuality, or the experiencing of difficulties with the opposite sex, is the result of more neutrally-
alike energies attempting through sexuality to establish a
polarized set of opposite magnetic energies. Since opposite
magnetic energies attract more, it becomes obvious that
Homosexual sex must create more of a need for sexual expression while Heterosexual sex can because of the neut-
ralization of energies carry with it a measure of greater
fulfillment.

Now there is no question that an individual can have
many Retrogrades and not be homosexual. But the individual who experiences a Retrograde influence in his sexuality does go through the three Retrograde phases, during
which in Phase I he over-reacts to the future expectation of
the possibility of engaging in sexual activity (overly early
and out of proportion in extent, based on future reality).
Then he is caught in the cross vibration of Phase II where
the act becomes somewhat of a let-down since he has already
experienced it in consciousness (and in some cases may even
be impotent because he has used up too much energy in
expectation). Finally, he becomes afraid of himself during
Phase III where he realizes he has overextended his own
limits and then timidly retraces his steps back into himself.
Literally, he has moved from extroversion during Phase I to
complete introversion during Phase III. Many cases of sexual failure, whether homosexual or heterosexual, are because of this kind of Regrograde influence.* If the threefold

* See *The Astrology of Sexuality*, M. Schulman, Samuel Weiser, Inc., York
Beach ME, 1982.

Retrograde process causing time and space warps were not enough to confuse the individual with many Retrograde planets, there is still another factor which is fairly common, and that is the turning inward of naturally outer-directed energies.

The more Retrogrades an individual has, the more he grows introspective and develops an entire other life within himself which often can be opposed to the life he has to live outwardly for the sake of the society whose acceptance he needs. What he understands about himself, and the world is often beyond expression to others.

When energies that are normally directed outward are turned inward, the individual begins to personalize the universe outside of him. In some ways he finds it difficult to really know where he ends and the universe beyond himself begins. As a result, he often gets hurt, by taking into himself more than he has to. Realizing his sensitivities to his environment he gradually builds walls around himself. Then, after he has retreated behind these walls he can sort out all of his problems, but he cannot necessarily communicate what he knows to people in the outer environment he has chosen to retreat from. His strongest contact with society is during Phase I when he is expanding himself in an attempt to reach outward, forward, and beyond his normal life experience.

RETROGRADES AND THOUGHT PROJECTION

One of the most fascinating aspects of Retrogrades occurs on an unconscious level. The individual projects the energies of his Retrogrades onto every individual with whom he communicates. But he does this in such a subtle way, that it is practically all but invisible to the conscious observer.

What actually happens is, he telepaths thoughts by subtly slipping into the identity of the person he is talking to. And while part of him remains in himself, another part stays in the other person's psychic space. Momentarily the other individual loses his own identity and begins to assume the thoughts, desires, and wishes of the Retrograde individual as if they were his own. Meanwhile what is actually happening is that the Retrograde person is really talking to himself.

If he has Karma that he does not wish to deal with, then he sees it being fed back to himself through the other person who has now become a mirror. Unfortunately he is usually unaware of this, and believes that it is the other person who is the originator of negative expression.

In those instances where the Retrograde individual has very positive or elevated Karma in his Retrograde planets, he can actually transfer the awarenesses he has reached to other individuals through this process of thought projection. Thus, he can be quite a mystical teacher on very subliminal levels.

The question must be asked, however, "How long does this juxtaposition stay before each individual reassumes his full original identity?" In the case of what appears to be negative Karma being exchanged, it will depend entirely upon how much the non-Retrograde individual is willing to assume. And in the case of positive Karma being exchanged it will depend entirely upon how long the individual feels that he needs whatever awarenesses he has received.

In both cases the transference of Karma usually lasts until the individual reaches his own truth about the matter, for once he does, whether the exchange was negative or positive, he can re-assume his own identity enriched by the experience.

It is interesting to note how these thought projections actually take place. Through the Retrograde individual's words or actions, the non-Retrograde individual begins to experience what he believes to be his own emotions, be it enthusiasm, joy, pain or sorrow, concerning the nature of the topic of the thought being projected.

Once an individual begins to feel something emotionally, he logically thinks that it is his own emotions, and therefore he must somehow act on it. So it becomes clear that the entire process of thought projection only works where unconscious "identification" is possible between two people.

In actual fact, a great deal of Karma is interchanged in

this fashion and whether or not it actually puts the human race through more pain and work than it really needs is a question only God can answer. But on an individual basis, it gives the person a chance to either consciously or unconsciously decide how much outside help he wants to ingest in order to solve his inner problems or how much interference he allows himself to receive which acts as a hindrance to seeing himself clearly. Ultimately he must decide for himself.

As an interesting note, it becomes possible for the Astrologer with some practice to know on an instinctive level exactly what planets an individual has Retrograde by what parts of himself he seems to be losing as he speaks to the individual.

RETROGRADES AND OBSESSIVE THOUGHTS

The threefold Retrograde Process causes an individual to relive all he experiences. This tends to trap the mind in a constant "echo-like" repetition of thought patterns. In an attempt to get over this, the person may verbalize all that is bothering him to others, but by doing so, he creates still more circumstances which will again be repeated in the future. In this manner, the chain becomes endless. Thus, it is much easier for a Retrograde planet to be the instigator of possessive thoughts or actions than for such behavior to be coming from any direct-motion planet.

This result of the Retrograde thought process is particularly apparent in the constant repetition of neurotic phobias, which echo themselves for years after the fear object is no longer present in the person's life. It is interesting to note how individuals with Retrograde Neptune tend to fear large bodies of water, being hypnotized, and getting involved too deeply in anything whose outcome is unclear. At the same time, people with Retrograde Pluto usually have unconscious sexual inhibitions accompanied by a death fear which does not allow them to enjoy the richness of sexual surrender. The Retrograde Saturn is not particularly fond of closed-in places, while Retrograde Jupiter sometimes exhibits acrophobia (fear of open spaces).

The interesting thing about Retrogrades is that for whatever role they play in stimulating and perpetuating phobias they also represent the easiest cure. All the individual needs to know is that whatever he is thinking in regard to his fears, is nothing more than the repeat echo of what he has thought before. And, he has perfect free will not to react to such an echo. When this is realized, a whole new behavior pattern is possible. But each time the individual allows himself to react to the echo of a past fear, he creates a new expereince which only gives birth to future echoes through the Retrograde repeat process. Naturally, this makes the fear more difficult to overcome.

Many habits are rooted in the Retrograde Process in exactly this manner. The individual keeps responding to the echoes of previous thoughts but he thinks he is responding to the original thought each time. And, every time he does this, he makes the echo the original experience, because he thinks it is so. This only makes him susceptible to responding to future echoes of the same thought. Many smokers have Retrograde Neptune in their charts, and all they have to do to break the smoking habit is to stop reacting to the echoes of the images that quickly flash in front of them just prior to reaching for a cigarette.

In overcoming negative ideas, feelings or beliefs, that are occurring as a result of the Retrograde Repeat Process, all the individual has to do is refuse to make echoes his reality. In time they disappear, and in their place he discovers that he truly does have control over his own being.

RETROGRADES AND SPIRITUAL GROWTH

The most amazing thing about Retrogrades is that for all the personal difficulties they cause an individual to experience in his private life, they are his spiritual keys towards the resolution of Karmic thought entities. All of us experience dualities in our identity systems. A part of us is the "me" while another part of us — the part society, tradition, and our parents have taught us — is the "not me". Still, because of training and a desire for acceptance in the outer world of appearance, this "not me" identity is fairly strong in most people. It not only causes judgemental attitudes, fears, and inhibitions, but almost tempts and dares the "me" identity to express itself.

The moment an individual realizes these two parts of himself and learns to separate all he has sacrificed in order to build his "not me" identity from his true "me" identity he has taken the first step towards understanding his real cosmic nature. People with Retrograde planets have the greatest ability to see these differences in themselves because through the introspective nature of the Retrograde (by way of whatever planet or house experience it represents) they begin to reach the "me" identity. Meanwhile, the outer world of tradition and appearance has difficulty understanding this supposed "black sheep" because of the uniquely different ideas and philosophies the individual stands for. At the same time, there is hardly a person he makes contact with who is not secretly (in his "me" identity) envious of the individual who has actually broken from living the "not me" life.

Thus, through one's Retrogrades, it is possible to ultimately become one's own Guru through the enormous self awareness that emerges the minute the "not me" identity is no longer a strong vibratory force in the person's life.

PART TWO

THE RETROGRADE PLANETS

RETROGRADE MERCURY

Retrograde Mercury
Esoteric Symbol

Traditionally Mercury has been ascribed the position of ruling all forms of communication. Its symbol (☿) formed by the circle of Spirit resting between the crescent of Soul and the Cross of Matter shows that man achieves union between these three essential parts of himself by understanding how they integrate in all of his creative expression. The crescent on top symbolizes the Soul which is actively pouring itself downward into Spirit which in turn strives to express itself outwardly by pushing its ideas downward further into the Cross of Matter. In order for this process to work, man must achieve the understanding that all knowing comes from the highest plane and gradually sifts down to the lowest. When man is in tune with himself all of his knowledge originates in his Soul and then by penetrating his Spirit seeks its outward expression through the actions of his body and his responses to the body of form he sees in the world around him. Thus, man's expression is greatly dependent upon his perception of things, as well as his Spirit, or his body. And perception is very much under the domain of Mercury's rulership.

As such, man can use his Mercury to experience his Soul, express his Spirit or fulfill the needs of his body. He may actively express himself based entirely upon his Divine Essence and thereby view the whole world as the experience of Soul in all things. Or he may seek to actively express himself through his Spirit, thereby coloring his perception of the world around him as a vivid moving kaleidoscope of life. Or his third possibility is that he may seek to use all expression in terms of fulfilling his physical needs. Therefore, he may see the world around him as material and physical.

The full man is able to do all of these. But most individuals choose one way of expression as superior to the other two.

When Mercury appears Retrograde the natural priority of Soul over Spirit over Matter becomes inverted. The individual is most concerned with the form of his life as well as understanding the form of all things around him. Then, through his perception of whether such form either fits or contradicts the ideas of form he established in himself through prior incarnations he reacts in Spirit. Finally when form is satisfied, and Spirit is activated he achieves contentment with form and allows himself to experience his Soul.

It is this trinity of Soul, Spirit and Matter that makes Mercury the most important planet in terms of how an individual perceives his total life experience.

RETROGRADE MERCURY PERSONALITY

When Mercury appears Retrograde in the horoscope, the individual's conscious mind is capable of tapping ideas in the universal consciousness from prior times. Usually, he is unaware he is doing this, but what he is aware of is that he cannot easily make others understand all he knows. In part this is because of the inversion of Mercury's symbol in which the importance of matter takes precedence over Spirit and Soul. This causes the individual to become preoccupied with the form of his ideas. And this acts as a block to the essence of his knowledge.

In addition, his wave length is slightly different from the rest of society in terms of his mental life. Thought processes tend to repeat like an endless record, and as a result most of the things he creates are in different shapes or forms, carbon copies of what he has already done. When he speaks, he has difficulty projecting the exact telepathic pictures which convey the meanings of his thoughts. Thus, he often feels misunderstood and wonders why others do not always see things the way he does.

He believes himself more separated from society than a person with direct-motion Mercury might. And as a result, he tries desperately to develop contact with others to the point that he often overemphasizes his ideas until they can actually become an annoyance to those around him. Uncomfortable in company, he tries too hard to win the acceptance of others. Still at the slightest hint of rejection, he can give up too easily. Ultimately he learns that his safety is in growing more detached and impersonal than those people with direct-motion Mercury. This is often interpreted by others as a "coldness" but it is merely the vibration of the Retrograde Mercury which is so obviously disharmonious with direct-motion vibrations. Underneath the apparent wall, this indivdidual is a lot more sensitive than most people would realize.

Once the communication barrier is passed, there is a tremendous amount of insight that comes out of the Retrograde Mercury. To make this easier, the Retrograde individual should not try to make the form of his life fit into the ideas and opinions of others around him. Instead he can find more comfort in being grateful for his rather unique way of seeing things.

It is interesting to note that there have been many great musical geniuses with Mercury Retrograde. Perhaps their awareness of difficulties with spoken language led them to another form of communication which had greater freedom and more levels of subtle mental and emotional expression.

In areas which require concentration, this individual can be an excellent student even though it may take him a little longer to grasp ideas and principles. In the end he will know the subject more thoroughly and with much greater insight and depth than the individual with direct-motion Mercury. This occurs because he literally ignores nothing. In areas of learning he is unwilling to skip over a point that leaves him questioning. Regardless of the impatience of others in a classroom situation he will constantly go back to some past question until the answer rests clearly.

He is a natural in the study of history, where the backwards study of man's nature gives an understanding of how one might predictably act in the future. Liking to teach others through his different sense of perspective, he has the ability to make one aware of past details that are needed in the present in order to recapture and put together puzzle pieces which would otherwise be missing. To do this, he always seems to be fighting the natural flow of things, which leads him to be misunderstood by those close to him. This causes nervousness and irritability when enough of a buildup triggers feelings of separation from those he wishes to be close to.

Because he is drawing on overlooked but still useful ideas from the past, he tends to come into contact with those individuals who are running ahead into the future so fast that they are missing many pieces behind them. He can fill this gap for them, as soon as they stop to listen.

Dealing with different time periods all at the same time, the Retrograde Mercury individual is acting like a funnel and an interpreter. Always there is a powerful message, but he will shy away from giving it unless he feels accepted at the moment.

In the area of sexuality, this placement makes it difficult to establish smooth flowing communication with the opposite sex. In some instances it can indicate homosexuality, particularly if it forms conjunctions or squares to Mars, Venus or Neptune, or if it is placed in the Eighth house forming any aspect to Uranus.

RETROGRADE MERCURY
KARMA

The individual with Retrograde Mercury is here to experience an unresolved Karma in relationships. He has a tendency to react to others as if they symbolize people from his past. Thus, he has difficulty keeping the full focus of his consciousness in the "here and now."

Usually this manifests as difficulties with family and relatives. But the question of relationships goes beyond how one communicates with people. It also involves one's perception of the universe as a whole. Often there is a problem inherent in the Retrograde Mercury in terms of seeing what might be called an inverted reality. The individual has difficulty understanding the very basic relationship between cause and effect. He questions the very essence of life itself, yet he cannot often see the most simple links between things, circumstances, and people. Losing himself in thought which is beyond comprehension he must learn to be content with the very basic simplicities upon which life is founded. So intent is he on discovering that which is beyond understanding that he nearly always misses the obvious.

From a Karmic point of view then, this individual must learn how to focus his attention on the reality of the present rather than losing himself in all of the transparent overlays he perceives. Once he can do this, he will be able to establish a firm reference point in the here and now through which all of the discoveries he makes can be expressed to the outer world.

RETROGRADE MERCURY IN ARIES

Here the individual is most comfortable during Phase I, where his thirst for understanding is rushing him forward through the Cardinal, Martian qualities of Aries, so that he re-experiences a primitive part of his thought development from former incarnations. All of his thought and sensory patterns reflect his almost child-like desires to prove his mental competence.

Lacking in patience he often experiences poor judgement through impulsive thinking. This puts him out of time sequence with most people he talks to. Still, this individual is a strong debater, enjoying the challenge of mental stimulation. This enables him to prove himself worthy, even though the reasons for his thinking himself inadequate are not coming from this life. Constantly wondering if he is good enough in the eyes of the world, he races forward to prove that he can meet the challenges of his past. Interestingly enough, the individuals whose understanding he originally wanted are no longer in the picture.

The Retrograde Mercury is most out of harmony with the sign Aries during Phase III where the individual is going back in consciousness to re-experience that which he has already lived through. It is for this reason that this individual hates repeating himself and complains actively about having to live in a world which loses its intellectual stimulation by constantly reconsidering actions it has already completed.

RETROGRADE MERCURY
IN TAURUS

Here the individual is most comfortable in Phase III, where the absorbing qualities of Venus-ruled Taurus allow him to dwell in the secure comfort of understanding a past he has already lived through. He is a slow and careful thinker. And, even after completing action, he mentally goes back to it to be sure he was right. Sometimes he fixates on a thought for so long that the idea actually becomes an obsession. Always he is conscious of the feelings of language rather than the mental interpretation of it. And, in an effort to convey these feelings he will attach more ego-importance to words than they may actually be worth. This being his most negative quality is characteristic of Phase I where he is the least comfortable. He doesn't like to impress himself outwardly on others, for although he may have exaggerated inner feelings of self-importance he is really quite introverted.

Still, this individual has great aspiration to achieve much mental growth, and he is willing to work hard for it. Shunning much that would come easy, he prefers the long, sure and steady road.

His worry over money and fears about the future are Karmic symbols of problems he has already lived through in the past. Now he is reliving all of his thoughts of insecurity in an attempt to convince himself that he is safe. He often talks to himself so that by hearing the inner sound of his voice he will eventually come to believe in his own sureness. He likes to think that all he has lived through has been logical, practical, and part of a growth pattern which makes sense to him. Perhaps his greatest strength coming from past incarnations is that he knows how to be a builder in form, and he can be highly constructive to other individuals during Phase I where he outwardly expresses his ideas to exactly those people who need to know how to put ideas together.

RETROGRADE MERCURY IN GEMINI

Here, the individual experiences the mutable adaptibility of Gemini as it acts on Retrograde Mercury moving through its three phases. Because of the dual nature of the sign, and its intense quest for understanding, along with a chameleon-like changeability according to external influence, this individual is able to experience comfort during each one of the three Retrograde phases.

Actually, he is on different thought planes at the same time. This ability to experience different frequencies of thought simultaneously makes it possible for him to deal with hypocrisy better than any other zodiacal placement. He can be an unusually agile communicator even though his thoughts sometimes seem a bit disjointed. This is because, although he can have difficulties pulling things together, he has a great ability to see the essence of an idea instantly.

He is good at writing poetry and music, but sometimes gets himself into mental mazes by attempting to test his thinking powers.

In some instances there is past life residue of a relationship with a brother or a sister. And, when obvious difficulties in that area continue in the present life, he still keeps trying to resolve the past incarnation by working it out through the present actors. His Karma is in relationships with others, and all he goes through in this life is part of his learning to understand the nature of duality within himself. His greatest strength is the fact that he is a born student, and while it may take him longer to learn something than the individual with direct-motion Mercury, he will ultimately understand it on a deeper level.

RETROGRADE MERCURY IN CANCER

In this placement, the individual experiences his greatest harmony during Phase III where he is able to absorb the consciousness of all other individuals who bring him back to reenacting through his memory the thoughts of all he has experienced. His mind and emotions are so linked, that all thought creates feeling and all feeling creates thought. Both are so deeply rooted in past experience that he keeps trying to recreate his childhood. Because of this, upbringing is important, for many childhood experiences will be carried as residue all through the life.

This person is emotionally sensitive and needs independence of thought with emotional security at the same time. This is a difficult balance to achieve for if he leans on others for security, he loses his independence of thought, he will lose the emotional security that he gained by leaning on others. His easiest bargain is to grow emotionally possessive of his thoughts, which, unfortunately, can lead him into many neurotic complexes that he finds himself unable to let go of. It is very difficult for him to bury the past and move ahead into the future free and clear. Because he analyzes his emotions rather than letting them flow, he actually can give power to negative emotional states making them larger than they really are without even realizing it.

He has brought with him into this incarnation many dependency thoughts from the past. And it is through these thoughts that he keeps re-enacting child-parent roles with everyone he relates to. Seeking both emotional and mental fulfillment at the same time, he is incomplete when receiving one without the other. He does not fully understand the concept of growth and keeps thinking himself incapable of letting go of earlier phases in his life. In his later years, he develops a very beautiful rapport with children, which eventually turns out to be one of his greatest strengths.

RETROGRADE MERCURY
IN LEO

The greatest harmony between the planet and the sign in this placement is found in Phase I of the Retrograde Process. Here the individual seeks to outwardly radiate his authoritative knowledge to others in order to try to power the future now. He keeps trying to think of how he can conquer tomorrow's obstacles. In his enthusiasm he may have a strong tendency to exaggerate. Being formidably proud, he is silently jealous of all large accomplishments that he personally hasn't had a hand in.

He is the least comfortable during Phase III where he does not feel a participant in all he sees going on around him.

Past-life thoughts of power keep seeping into the conscious mind, making him desirous of achievements. In fact, at times he thinks he is being pressured into achieving. This was probably true in one of his past incarnations, but mistaking the past for the present, he tries to apply pressure to his conscious thinking in this life too. He likes the attention he receives from others during Phase I and misses it greatly during Phase III where his inner pride prevents him from asking for his needs. Truly he is also not completely comfortable in Phase I because his Leonian honesty prevents him from blowing his own horn prematurely. Thus, whichever phase he experiences, he tends to hold much inside. Although past incarnations have taught him to think big enough to transcend narrow frameworks or small ideas, it is the frustration of the Retrograde Process that makes it difficult for him to always be able to express what he knows. His greatest asset is his ability to evaluate the totality of situations where others see only glimpses.

RETROGRADE MERUCRY IN VIRGO

Here the individual experiences the benefits of planetary rulership through which the mutable qualities of Virgo blend with Mercury's infinite curiosity to enable a degree of comfort in all three Retrograde Phases. The least harmony with the sign occurs in Phase I where the individual is trying to leap ahead of himself, but cannot yet make all he wants to do a reality. This explains the extreme nervousness found during the first phase. As a result, there is a tendency to stay in Phase II slightly longer, where the individual can manifest that which is familiar to him. Then during the final phase he displays his overly critical tendencies as he looks back at all that was completed, studying its flaws and matching it against the ideal in his mind.

He can appear to be on the strict, cold side displaying little tolerance for disorder. He also has strong opinions for what is right and wrong in terms of how others should live their lives. Still he shies away from the tightness of entangling relationships, feeling much more comfortable when there is a slight distance between himself and those around him. While not being a particularly warm Mercury placement for personal relationships, this position does give the individual the abilities of a highly skilled, impartial thinker.

In past incarnations, he underwent experiences which taught him a particular method of thinking of how to figure out all the intricacies within himself and the universe. He learned to see a major gap between how the world works in reality and how it could work in his ideals. He has discovered that machinery of all kinds can be closer to the ideals he saw than the machinery of human relationships. Thus, in all his dealings with people he tries to make everything fit into these computer-like ideals established many years in the past. His joy comes from his confidence in solving problems which involve details that others are unable to handle. He may not have many friends, but those who are close to him will be discriminately hand-picked.

RETROGRADE MERCURY
IN LIBRA

This is one of the more difficult positions for a Retrograde Mercury. During Phase I and III the individual feels himself to be out of balance with Libras's delicate need for centering. During Phase II, when he experiences a little bit of the past along with the present, as well as slight hints that in the future he will be coming back to exactly where he is now, he can be more in harmony with Libra's basic qualities. Staying in this phase the longest accounts for his very strong feeling of non-direction.

He brings into this life a Karma of indecisiveness in his thought processes, and as he keeps tipping the scale from one side to the other, people close to him hardly understand what he stands for. At the same time, not being sure of the directions his decisions take him, he is always interested in knowing how people in his past would approve or disapprove of the decisions he makes now.

At times he can be extremely contrary, and if the Retrograde Mercury is badly aspected, even dishonest. He values tact and diplomacy above truth. It is interesting to note that the dictionary definition of the word "tact" is "insincerity."

In the present life, this individual experiences conflict with his parents, and as an adult keeps thinking that he has to create harmony with them. In fact, he tries to do this to everyone he meets. Still he confuses his thinking and feeling levels and he can be fearful of self-expression. He often thinks that by expressing himself he would not be accepted by those whose love he wants. This can lead him to see the world through rose-colored glasses, with a leaning towards the avoidance of being personally responsible for his thoughts. As a result, he has difficulty knowing his own identity. But the interesting thing is, that this is exactly what enables him to be of great assistance in balancing others, as he from moment to moment puts himself in one person's place and then another to understand situations from all possible points of view.

RETROGRADE MERUCRY IN SCORPIO

Here the individual experiences his best union during Phase I, where Mercury's need for activity blends with Scorpio's quest for discovery in agitating the individual enough so that he develops strong desires to move ahead into areas as yet unknown to him. As a result, he develops an unusually keen mind with the ability to keep reviewing (during Phase III) in order to find the depths of things that others have overlooked. He is capable of re-discovering that which has been buried in the past. This makes him a natural at anything of a scientific nature.

An unusually deep individual, he is fully capable of solving his own problems. Thus, he tends to be more on the silent side, rarely ever verbalizing anything that bothers him. At the same time, his conscious mind can be destructive when he observes things that do not live up to his idealistic expectations.

He can be sexually detached and lack the warmth that others expect of him on the sexual level. At the same time he can also get himself sexually preoccupied on the mental level.

There was much past-life upheaval in the conscious experience. Now the individual must draw on the energy of that upheaval to keep his present awarenesses from slipping into any negative experiences. Thus, he can be suspicious of others, shrewd, and tactless, but he is a truth seeker at all costs. With this placement, the conscious mind works best when focused on the spiritual journey.

Many with Retrograde Mercury in Scorpio have experienced separation from a loved one at a young age in a former incarnation. This helps to make it possible for such individuals to be able to stand strongly in this life, carrying somewhat of an inner loneliness which only strenghens their individuality.

RETROGRADE MERCURY IN SAGITTARIUS

This is truly a lost soul that needs much help from others if he is to find himself in the great expanses of his mental wanderings. In other incarnations he had been a seeker, but his meanderings have still not established a central frame of reference within which he can catalogue his information. He still tries to cover so many subjects that he often doesn't know where to start speaking, or what is truly relevant to talk about.

This placement makes concentration difficult, for as the individual tries to deeply focus on a particular topic, his thoughts are always interrupted by external distractions which make him feel that whatever he is thinking about is hardly worthy of much attention. Thus, he leaves many problems in life unsolved. He gains much from Earth signs, for they offer the stability he needs.

His biggest difficulty is that his mind wants to comprehend everything under heaven in order to take the information back to some past time and apply it to a problem as yet unresolved. The difficulty here is that the information acquired is usually superficial and scattered to the point where it is too difficult for him to apply in any one area. Unfortunately he keeps trying to use the impersonal Jupiterian wisdoms which reflect the great cosmic truths to his own personal problems in the past, rather than rising his present life personal self to a cosmic level.

He does not like to have others impose thier thoughts on him, for he is using much of his mental independence to seek the rectification of a past injustice. Oddly enough, the Jupiterian effect is to scatter the Mercury enough so that it is impossible for him to do this, yet he keeps trying. Even when he comes into the present he tends to exaggerate all of these thoughts out of proportion to the realities they respresent.

In this sign Mercury experiences difficulties during all three phases of the Retrograde Process. It never has the opportunity to experience enough of a stabilizing influence to make clear and precise thinking a natural way of life.

In spite of all of this however he is oddly enough a very mystical spiritual messenger to everyone he meets.

RETROGRADE MERCURY IN CAPRICORN

This individual is a very deep and weighty thinker. Having once made a mistake he has the ability to understand it on a deep level with a great sense of perspective. He can then approach the source or a similar construct again and make it work correctly.

In his early years he seems to do things the hard way, but this helps him to achieve much later on. Self expression is difficult for him, for he tries too hard to pinpoint his exact meaning. Thus, he only likes to talk about things that are either meaningful, serious, or which represent sobriety. He does not live a spontaneous life, for it is easier for him to be more in tune with the purpose of his own thought patterns, than the natural flow of forces in the world around him. In all things, he always considers the end result before he will even contemplate the steps he might take towards achieving it. Thus, he is highly pragmatic and practical.

Bringing with him into this incarnation the knowledge of how man attains his physical goals in substance, he knows the steps that must be taken to achieve anything substantial, and will draw on this past-life knowledge again and again in order to try to convey this to others who are always looking for the easy way out. He is more easily understood later in life after the weight of his thinking has found suitable outlets in traditional society. In the first half of life he can go through paranoid periods in which he gets bogged down in his own depth. Still, he is more than able to plod his way back out.

His greatest difficulties lie in personal relationships as others tend to lose patience with all he is trying to build. Still, the greatest strength of this position occurs during Phase III of the Retrograde Process where seeing his crystallized thoughts from the past, he is able to absorb more knowledge for future building.

RETROGRADE MERCURY IN AQUARIUS

This is one of the best positions for Retrograde Mercury. The Uranian airy quality of Aquarius allows Mercury ample room to experience the threefold Retrograde Process comfortably through different dimensions of time and space. In Phase I, the individual is happy about jumping into the future but does not want to expand into other people's space. During Phase III, he is happy about not violating other people's space, and he is not unhappy about reexploring the past in order to dig up strange discoveries that will be useful in still another future moment. In the cross vibration of Phase II, he experiences a momentary rest from his explorations, but he can be happy about helping others. Thus, through all three phases, there is something for this Retrograde Mercury in Aquarius that makes the individual so beautifully unique, and original.

Although he may not always appear to have common sense, and sometimes displays less stability than others would want to see in him, he has a tremendous scope of ideas coming from the most out of the way places that society usually chooses to overlook. He may draw on a concept as old as the hills, changing it slightly into an idea that may not be accepted for a thousand years after he has proposed it. His mental energies flit about rather than holding a specific focus for any long period of time, and he can discuss a wide variety of subjects in a single conversation. While he may not seem to be making a point, he does make his point in the strangest of ways. And, he is more understood by others — days, weeks or months after they have been in his presence rather than at the exact moment of specific contact. He is so inventive that he often carries with him the necessary details for great ingenuity from a past life into the present time where the world may be more ready to accept his ideas.

RETROGRADE MERCURY IN PISCES

With this placement, the individual can experience much confusion in the conscious mind. He keeps thinking he is lost and yet cannot readily put his finger on the keynote of his feeling. In a past incarnation he experienced a great desperation in his thoughts. Now he keeps recreating those same circumstances and events which allow him to re-enact this desperation so that somehow he might finally find the solution he has been seeking. He will discover that he can only find his answers when he is aware of the questions he is asking

One of his difficulties is that he has trouble separating mental energies from intuition. Losing himself in imagination, thoughts and fantasies, he can become out of contact with the sharpness of reality. Often he thinks that others do not understand the scope of the ideas he is trying to express. He may know and understand things that are simply beyond words, but when he tries to express this with language he feels he has literally lost the essence of the idea.

Bringing with him into this incarnation a sense of cosmic idealism, that he finds difficult to explain, he experiences just conflict between joining the world as he sees it now and desiring to escape it. He does not really think of himself as being truly worthy of others' acceptance, and yet at the same time, he wonders if the values of social acceptance represent any reality at all.

He is most comfortable in Retrograde Phase III where in his absorbing vibration he can ponder on all he has already lived through. His least amount of comfort is during

Phase II where through the actual living out of all he has already had past glimpses of, he is afforded the poorest opportunity for the expression of his imagination and creative originality.

RETROGRADE MERUCRY IN THE FIRST HOUSE

Here, the individual is most comfortable in Phase I of the Retrograde experience where thought is focused on the expectation of self-progress. He is impatient, with tendencies to jump to conclusions which later need to be corrected. The entire horoscope takes on a child-like quality as many of the planetary energies are redirected inward to a focus on the self.

This position tends to bring the individual into association with those who are young and immature. He brings into this incarnation a very basic elemental Karma in his self-development. Not fully understanding how to focus his mental energies outward, he becomes a part of all he thinks he projects. Thus, he has difficulty knowing where he ends and the outer world begins. Like a child, he needs attention, but he doesn't always know what to do with it when he gets it. He stampedes into situations only to retreat into himself once he is there. His biggest problem is finding out who he really is, for he is sifting through a Karma of constantly questioning his self-identity. And again like a child, he is highly impatient to find out. Never waiting for the understanding of the world to come to him, he rushes into it to know all he can — yesterday.

Still he has difficulty measuring what he knows when he finds what he thinks he has been looking for.

The Astrologer should expect a slight imbalance in all the other planets in the horoscope with this position, as Mercury's focal lens for expressing all their energies is subject to the threefold Retrograde Process.

RETROGRADE MERCURY IN THE SECOND HOUSE

Here the individual is most comfortable during Phase

III where much of his thoughts are built upon that which he has already seen in the past. He can be defensive of the value systems he has worked so hard to crystallize. Easily growing possessive of his past thoughts he can fixate himself in one obsession after another.

Much attention is focused on money and yet he can be penny-wise and pound foolish, depending upon which phase he is in at the moment. The difficulty in this position is that the thought processes can become so deeply rooted in matter that the individual has difficulty seeing the relative importance of other levels in life.

He tends to repeat himself a great deal, eventually boring those around him. This is a very difficult position for Mercury to be free enough to allow the individual to experience his full range of conscious response mechanisms. In nearly all he does he is a creature of habit and he often experiences difficulties breaking any past behavior patterns associated with overindulgence. Sometimes this position can lead to overweight, as Retrograde Mercury's need for oral expression, combined with the Second Houses's possessive qualities, and ruling Taurus' great love of food creates desires for overeating. In other instances, the holding qualities of the Second House combine with Retrograde Mercury's turning inward to produce the ulcer-prone individual who rather than expressing all his values, aggravates himself over why the world will not accept them

This is the individual who brings with him in this life a crystallized thought Karma in his value systems, which he is stubbornly holding onto long after its expression is appropriate in the world. He can be the happiest of people once he transcends old worn out habit patterns that have been constantly pulling him down.

RETROGRADE MERCURY
IN THE THIRD HOUSE

Here, Retrograde Mercury appears in the house it rules. As such, it experiences a good amount of flexibility as it moves through its three phases. The individual is highly mentally active, and focuses much of his chart energies on trying to be understood by others. He often inhibits his total expression if he feels others will take what he is saying the wrong way. Still, he has much he would like to say. When he experiences Phase III, he spends much energy going back over thoughts to be sure they were expressed to others exactly the way he meant to express them.

His greatest difficulties occur in his relationships with others as he tries to synchronize his understandings with those around him. Sometimes there is a family problem with a brother or sister.

With this placement, the individual brings into the cur-·rent life a strong relationship Karma. And, since he is always studying the relationships between all things and people in his life, he is constantly switching his wavelength according to what he senses around him. Sometimes this can cause stuttering or hamper mental expression. Thus, in spite of a flexible mentality, he has great difficulty flowing in smooth patterns as he tries to express what he knows. He can bog himself down in the use of language by constantly seeking to find the right word that will say all he wants to convey. Then, after he has spoken, he will test the reaction to what he has said to know if he should jump into another Retrograde Phase or stay longer in the one which might be proving successful. Still, he is one of the most analytical thinkers of the Zodiac.

RETROGRADE MERCURY
IN THE FOURTH HOUSE

Here, the individual is most comfortable during Phase III where he can absorb all that has represented past memories of security. Thus, he spends much of his time in this backward, introspective, absorbing phase where he feels the most safe.

His childhood was important as much of his thoughts now center around the feelings he experienced in those early years. He may think that the needs of others are holding him back, particularly those of his own family, but actually it is his need most of all to express himself in an environment where he is positively sure of himself. The outer world does not present such an environment. Thus, he doesn't always express the uniqueness of his identity and purpose through the right channels, but instead has a strong tendency to linger in child-like stages of complaining about why his life is not blossoming the way he thinks it should.

He brings into this incarnation a Karma that is holding his mental processes in earlier stages of his emotional development. Thus, it is only through his being born into new and higher emotional levels that afford him the security to express himself adequately on the mental plane.

He experiences confusion between dominance and submissiveness for he feels the Cardinal outpouring quality of the Fourth House and at the same time, he is emotionally so immature at expressing himself outwardly that he tends to take the entire conflict inside himself, thereby closing off his expression, except for more limited forms that do not entirely make him happy.

This is a very difficult position for the Retrograde Mercury for it colors the entire chart with past emotional thoughts, which dependent upon their nature, will either allow or impede the remainder of the horoscope to express itself.

RETROGRADE MERCURY IN THE FIFTH HOUSE

Here the individual is most comfortable in Phase I, although all three phases represent frustration in his life style. Experiencing difficulties in focusing his mental energies he is working on a Karma learning how to make his mental plane productively creative.

Curiosity leads him to leap ahead into the multitude of ideas that he would like to create. Yet it is much easier for him to think about creating or tell others what he would like to create than to actually carry out his projects completely.

He experiences great sexual tensions whose energies are constantly spilling over into his mental centers. Attracted to younger people, he finds it easier to express to them the radiating qualities of the first phase, rather than the natural introverted tendency of the Retrograde.

When he is in the company of people his own age or older he becomes more inhibited. Of all the twelve houses, this quality becomes more magnified here as the individual is confronted with conflict between being the actor at the center of his life or a spectator of it, through observing the actions of others.

He is attracted to reading romantic novels as well as stories of how people reached greatness but he has difficulty in putting his knowledge into practice. He often thinks he should be doing more than he is and this keeps his mind racing further and further into the future while the natural quality of Retrogrades to look back keeps receiving glimpses of how little he has accomplished in his past. He must learn how to overcome these frustrating mental pictures which keep impeding him in all he thinks he could be.

Some with this position are inclined to shy away from the opposite sex, as childhood problems are reprojected into individuals of the opposite sex in their present and future. In addition there is the tendency to project personal childhood inadequacies onto his own children.

The Karma in this placement is to be able to understand how to organize and create the present from all that the individual has been conscious of in the past.

RETROGRADE MERCURY
IN THE SIXTH HOUSE

Here Mercury finds itself in the house it rules. The mutable qualities of the Sixth House combine with the natural flexibility of Mercury to give the individual a keenly analytical approach to the organizatin of his life.

While he experiences a degree of comfort in all three phases he still undergoes difficulties in getting along with others, particularly in working situations. During Phase I he often tries to impress his ideas upon others, while in Phase III he critically goes back in time to analyze how well or poorly these ideas were put into practice. Because of others' reactions to him, he becomes highly nervous. Thinking that people expect things of him, he develops feeling of obligations to them. To organize his working habits he must understand the end result and back up to the beginning steps which will lead him to where he is going.

He can be overly critical of himself, spending much energy wondering whether he should keep judging his inner being or focusing his mental energies outward in an attempt to overcome his faults through service to others. Yet, there are times when others decline his service. Thus, he experiences frustrations in his dealings with people.

He is far better at organizing things than people. One of his biggest difficulties is that he has a tendency to harness his life to self-imposed restrictions. Sometimes he accepts responsibilities that he thinks he shouldn't, while shying away from those that he thinks he should. He brings forward into this life a Karma of discrimination, through which he is constantly trying to make all things and people fit into his preconceived order of the universe.

He is an excellent worker, especially in areas of following procedure created in the past. He must learn to become more tolerant of the human factor, so that his high ideals for order and perfection do not lead him into a negative attitude towards the people he works with and the society he lives in. He must one day come to see that he has a strong tendency to judge himself by his ideals at the same time as he judges others by their actions.

RETROGRADE MERCURY IN THE SEVENTH HOUSE

This is one of the most difficult positions for a Retrograde Mercury, as the individual's attempt at analyzing is always colored by what he sees through the eyes of others. Thus, he spends most of his time in Phase III going back and sorting out that which he has already lived through in terms of how well it balances with the likes and dislikes of those he loves. He experiences frustrations in the areas of marriage, career, and family as he seeks to keep going back and harmonize all of the ideas of people around him. He can feel anger at not being able to spend enough time thinking about himself. He is often misunderstood by those he is trying to explain things to because he tends to focus his energies more through their minds than his own. This causes him to be nervous in the presence of other people, and as a result, he doesn't always express himself to his best potential. His marriage mate can be on the childlike side, and in some instances she may actually be seeking the past qualities of a sister or brother in this mate.

He is highly indecisive, and unless other chart factors are very strong, has a tendency to lean on others for support because he is unsure of the decisions he makes for himself. At the same time, he can readily make decisions for others. He is often found in contrary situations, becoming the mediator to opposing points of view. Karmically, he is learning to balance the focus of his ideas through the needs of others around him. This hampers his self-expression, but at the same time greatly enhances his ability to understand others. He often goes back, re-evaluating ideas that others have skimmed over, seeing both sides of the picture and thus he is ultimately able to develop a fuller perspective. What makes this placement so difficult is that it tends to use its energies more in an impersonal way. Thus, it is better for use towards the externals of an individual's life rather than for intimate personal needs.

Of course, the frustration here is that Mercury is a personal planet and being Retrograde tends to be introverted. Yet here, in the Seventh House, it can neither function personally nor in an introverted manner.

RETROGRADE MERCURY IN THE EIGHTH HOUSE

Here, Mercury is highly energized by the Plutonian upheavals which bring endings to chapters in the indivdual's life. He spends much of his time in Phase III, constantly re-evaluating the ways in which he has regenerated himself into higher levels of consciousness. With this position he is an unusually deep thinker and his thought processes go right to the heart of life's essential meaning.

He may often experience sexual problems because the depth of his thinking makes him constantly question the value of all physical expression. He never accepts answers to his qustions on a superficial level, but rather seeks to know the ultimate why of all that exists. He has a tendency to shy away from intimate relationships with others. And even when involved, keeps much of his thoughts to himself, while silently observing the meaning of all that is around him.

He brings a legacy of seeking into this life, where he continually retraces the deepest meaning he can find to all he perceives. Sometimes he thinks he is alienated from society, and unless he is a highly evolved soul, he can easily become a product of destructive thoughts. And, if he does hold thoughts like this, he can actually magnify them by absorbing like thoughts from the universal consciousness during Phase III of the Retrograde Process.

He must learn how to transform his visions of the past, including those of his heritage and ancestry into more appropriate forms which combine with constructive actions now.

Karmically, he is a regenerator of human thought, and he must learn how to listen carefully to the words of advice he gives to others; for ultimately these very same words turn out to be his own guidance for himself.

REROGRADE MERCURY IN THE NINTH HOUSE

Here in the Ninth House, Mercury finds by far its most difficult position. Whether the individual is moving forwards or backwards, expanding or contracting in the dimensions of time or space, he is nevertheless too distantly removed from the center of all he sees to make his perception purely accurate. Thus, as he tries to blend the energies he is dealing with, he can actually become philosophical over matters of trivia, while treating as trivia the broad philosophical insights which represent the answers to his life. He has difficulty taking advice from others and tends to accentuate those fixed areas in his horoscope which allow him to retain his freedom of purpose. He is usually against all that binds, and in his racing to and fro he covers much more ground than he can personally use for himself. But this makes him a great giver of information to others, and while he himself may experience a great deal of confusion, he is for others a higher mind messenger from the past, trying desperately to coordinate all he sees into a language understandable to all he talks to.

He is highly independent, and rarely accepts traditional approaches to life. If used poorly, this placement can make the individual a mental or spiritual glutton, searching for more and more bits of information which never quite give him the wisdom he thinks he is looking for. He tends to be a poor organizer, presenting his thoughts in such a manner which makes it extremely difficult for others to understand him. Usually, he is trying to be on a spiritual journey, and yet he is so rooted in the mental plane, that all he experiences gets turned back into the lower mind where it loses most of its spiritual qualities.

Truly this is the kind of individual that could experience Nirvana and then by mentally repeating question after question analyze it to the point where it becomes stripped of its essential meaning. And, as a result, in many ways, this is the person who is being Karmically tested in overcoming his lower mind. The more he uses it, the less it works for him. He is aware of the many inconsistencies in his thoughts, but he has the attitude that it is more important for him to get all of these thoughts out, allowing future generations the opportunity to correct, sort, and categorize them, than if he were to hamper his expression by limiting the quantity of ideas that he is filled with. And yet, with this position he does not truly feel completely comfortable relating with others. While in Phase I, he tries to pour out the myriad of ideas to others, but when he is in Phase III, he likes to be alone, seeing others as an interference to his thinking. In Phase I, he can easily exaggerate the relevance of his ideas as he is expressing them outwardly, while in Phase III he can become depressed at the inner realization of what little importance they actually had. The Phase II experience is actually too centered for the Ninth House Retrograde Mercury to feel comfortable in for any given length of time.

In the midst of what seems to be very chaotic expression it should be noted that all that this individual says is important. But, it is up the the listener to discriminate what is more relevant than the bulk of information in terms of his own personal usefulness.

RETROGRADE MERCURY IN THE TENTH HOUSE

Here the individual is most comfortable in Phase III where he is able to reflect on past achievements, seeing how they measure up to all his expectations. All levels of conscious thought in this House are parent-oriented. The individual grows up with a great need to impress others and yet at the same time, inhibits his self-expression by his past training in propriety, prudence, and caution. He likes to see the practical outcome of his ideas and tends strongly to build his future in the same ways as he has built his past. He is always concerned with finding direction in life. In many instances he can be old for his years during the first part of life. Later on, he goes back to these early years to create his future. There is a strong need here to reabsorb past understandings coming from father.

Ultimately, he comes to place most of his self-identity in how successful he has been in terms of his ability to display wisdom to others. Thus, he seeks constantly to categorize his knowledge so that he can be sure that it will be ready for use whenever he may need it. He can experience much unhappiness in his personal life as he feels obligated to live up to past Karma of mental expectations. Nearly all he does in life is designed to establish in himself feelings of mental competence which ultimately becomes his main vehicle of self-confidence.

He tends to underrate himself silently, and as a result he keeps trying too hard to overcompensate. He wants to impress the inner parts of himself which are so overly hard to convince. As such, he is working on a Karma of trying to internally convince himself that his thoughts are constantly creating a direction which will bring him to ultimate feelings of worthiness.

RETROGRADE MERCURY IN THE ELEVENTH HOUSE

Here the individual experiences more mental freedom than he does the practical application of his thoughts. As he moves through the Retrograde Phases he can be an inspiration of ideas to others during Phase I, or at the other extreme, a complete daydreamer during Phase III, pondering over all he could have done, but didn't. The Uranian need for excitement and the mental need for stimulation makes Phase II the most uncomfortable for the individual, for it is during this period that he is at his lowest key. As a result, the combination of Phases I and III causes him to experience a great deal of impracticablity in his thinking. He finds it difficult to establish a sense of meaning. And yet, he finds it necessary to keep moving. He is in search of the unreachable, intangible rainbow that he believes actually exists. As a result he can well be the person who throws away a bird in the hand to go after two in the bush.

He is a loner, and yet he needs people, if only to add color to his ideas. At the same time, he has a way of remaining mentally detached. He can be cool and impersonal, avoiding close communication in intimate relationships. He doesn't like rigid ways of thinking on the part of others. It is more important for him to have freedom of mind than the ultimate result of how he applies it. He needs space to think, and is uncomfortable in crowds.

In some instances, he can be sexually unresponsive as he does not feel totally comfortable in intimate situations. He can pay lip service to marriage, children, and tradition, but his main strength is to be a disseminator of ideas to others. He finds it easy to personalize problems in society rather than dealing with those things which are closer at hand to his own life. Becoming indignant at social reforms long overdue, he can ignore personal reform within himself. Thus he experiences distortions in the priorities of his relationships to his society, his family and himself. He is a hard person for others to reach, for he can rebel against anything that binds him. Still, he is very much a universal seeker, focusing a great deal of his mental energies upon understanding the progress of the human race. He is intrigued by the process of evolution and mankind as a theory rather than as a fact. He doesn't like to confront the central core of life. Instead he is almost happy to view it as an outside observer. This tends to put the entire horoscope into a lifestyle of an individual who has a great deal of difficulty pointing his life in sensible directions through balanced means.

Karmically, he is engaged in studying levels of consciousness, without necessarily committing himself to any specific one. He compares past ideas with present realities and future dreams so that he may one day understand what it is that he thinks he is looking for. Without knowing the questions, he can hardly understand the answers, but he is still a seeker of the highest order, and he would do well to study the ways of Taoism or Zen, where some of his unconventional ideas can actually find a haven of truth on a universal level.

RETROGRADE MERCURY IN THE TWELFTH HOUSE

Here the individual spends most of his time in Phase III of the Retrograde Process, where in the absorbing introspective vibration he turns most of his thoughts inward to understand the inner nature of his own being. In this very special placement, every conscious thought is Karmic. All the individual perceives is a continuance of past ideas in his mind concerning the relationships of things, people and circumstances in the universe. He tends to draw into himself and on the personality level becomes introverted. Still, he is thinking all the time. He tends to replay past conversations for days and weeks after they have actually occurred. In a way he is experiencing the pure essence of perception in its rawest form. For most individuals this is very difficult to handle.

His frequent disorientation with time and space knows no boundaries, and often goes beyond the borderlines of the current life, as well as the planet he is currently living on. He can be mystically oriented as he tries to perceive the universe through himself. Thus, he tends to experience in his own life, any thing he allows himself to think about. Truly this is the individual who has become exactly "what he thought."

He is nearly always misunderstood by others, for the Neptunian essence of his ideas becomes awkward as he tries to express it to others through the absorbing introverted Phase III of the Retrograde Process.

He underestimates himself, tending to retreat from life rather than easily expressing himself outwardly. Some with this position have great musical ability, as words often seem inadequate means of expression, thereby leading the person to other creative areas of expressing themselves. On the negative side, some with this position can experience long periods of mental depression, during which time they are attempting to sort out the multitude of thoughts they are absorbing from the formless universe. This individual is here to Karmically understand himself on the very deepest of levels.

In order to do this, he spends much time away from the many outer world activities which would otherwise prevent him from seeing the seed of his inner being. Thus, he avoids the lighter side of life and focuses much of his attention on the deep mysteries that confront his inner mind.

He is quite a student of the past, and can become an excellent metaphysician when he directs his mental energies towards universal knowing.

RETROGRADE VENUS

RETROGRADE VENUS
ESOTERIC SYMBOL

Venus, the ruler of love, beauty and harmony, is symbolized by (♀) the circle of spirit over the cross of matter. Here the spirit in man pours down into expression in form, thus creating life. When form is created out of spirit it becomes something beautiful as all that man creates springs forth from his etheric nature. Through Venus, the beauty, harmony, and love in man's spirit can find their way into matter.

When Venus is Retrograde this progression, as with Mercury, becomes inverted, and man depends upon form to activate his spirit. Thus, if the material side of his life is inconsistent with his experiences with form in past incarnations, he tends to allow the spirit to negate all that exists in reality. With all Retrogrades, the form or material part of his life dominates as the individual keeps trying to understand all of the Karma he has crystallized into matter in past incarnations.

The individual with Venus Retrograde is less of an actor in life than he is a reactor to it. It is important to understand that the crescent of soul is missing from the Venus symbol and it is for this reason that Venus is ascribed to that very personal part of man's harmonizing nature while Neptune, containing the crescent of soul allows man to experience all beauty from its cosmic source. Wherever soul is present as a conscious force, the personal part of man is always subservient. Thus, we see so much giving manifested through Neptune. But, wherever soul is absent as a conscious force, the personal part of man's nature always takes precedence. This is why we see so much asking for personal fulfillment through Venus. The Retrograde nature enhances this to the point that the individual develops very strong reaction patterns to all that happens to him in life, judging each event, circumstance, and relationship in terms of how much he is being loved, or how much he is being denied love experiences.

Thus, the general effect of Retrograde Venus is felt mostly in that very personal side of life which is not fed through Soul, but rather an attempt at making form the mother of spirit. As a result, the material or physical side of life takes command.

RETROGRADE VENUS PERSONALITY

The personality of the Venus Retrograde individual is markedly different than that of the person with Venus in direct motion. There is a tendency to internalize hurts, working out within himself, what the direct motion Venus would try to work out externally. Often, the Retrograde Venus not only creates these hurts, but also tends to exaggerate their effect. There is an overemphasis on the imperfections of the love (or loves) in his life. For this person, the path of love does not flow smoothly.

Overly self-conscious, he usually wonders if others are paying as much attention to him as he is to himself. Not always positive about his likes and dislikes, he tends to experience a gap between living his life and experiencing the consciousness of it. He can be deeply in love and not know it until years after ending the relationship. He goes through many similar behavior patterns all designed to deny himself in reality what he thinks he truly needs.

There is always difficulty with the opposite sex as he tends to unconsciously pre-program his future relationships so that they fit into the patterns of his past.

A great deal of insecurity accompanies this position as the individual is constantly trying to align himself in ways which he feels will mesh with others. But, as he does this, he semi-consciously keeps pushing others away from him so that no one truly knows him deeply enough to threaten whatever little amount of security he has based his identity on. This position tends to make the life more lonely inwardly as the individual blocks himself from happiness by trying too hard to achieve it.

RETROGRADE VENUS
KARMA

When Venus is Retrograde, the individual is carrying with him a great misunderstanding about love in a past life. Usually there was such intense hurt, that he now cuts himself off from fully experiencing the richness of love because he fears being hurt that much again. Whether male or female, there is much present life difficulty in relationships with the opposite sex.

While trying to live in the present, he endlessly recreates a past memory of love in a former incarnation which still keeps eluding him. He reacts to the present as if he were actually living in his past. In this sense he is fixated at a point in time, and no matter what he does there hardly seems to be the forward progress that he says he wants.

In the charts of males, this sometimes indicates Karma related to homosexuality. But even homosexuality has its degrees, ranging from the outspoken male who tries politically to sell homosexuality to the world down to the male who would not even hear the word in his presence, is married, but seeks every possible opportunity to avoid females while proving his masculinity. This latter type of male is the kind of individual whose life revolves around his male friends, using the guise of associations, clubs, hobbies, and so on as an excuse for his avoidance of women. He can function respectably in society, but he is still a latent homosexual. Less often, we find similar reactions in the female with Retrograde Venus.

The most noticeable Karmic pattern is that the individual, whether male or female has a powerful tendency to mistrust most offers of love, feeling that the individuals making these offers usually have ulterior motives.

RETROGRADE VENUS
IN ARIES

Here the individual is most comfortable in Phase I where he lives in the expectancy of creating all feeling which will bring him self-esteem. Being very self-conscious, he constantly concerns himself with what others think or feel towards him. He can become defensive when he feels others are putting him on the spot. For this reason he tends to spend much time alone.

He is very sensitive to other people's conceptions of themselves, and when he feels that someone else's negative self-evaluation is likely to rub off on him, he will quickly run in another direction.

One of his difficulties is a tendency to jump to conclusions about his feelings. He preconceives his perceptions to the point where rather than flowing with what life has to offer, he formulates his feelings about certain experiences before he has even experienced them. Still, he seeks experiences to test if his formulas were correct.

Marriage for this person is not an easy task for a general lack of trust combined with too much self-involvement prevents him from experiencing the full richness of another individual on an intimate basis. The boredom he usually feels is not a boredom with life or with other people, but rather an intense boredom with himself. Rather than face and understand this, he often takes great pains to fill his life with one distraction after another until he is convinced that he has nothing to do with his problem. The day he learns to like himself, his whole life changes.

He is working towards overcoming a past Karma in which he established a separation between his own feelings and the collective feelings of others. It is the residue of this subtle alienation from people that keeps him running from himself until he realizes that his entire construction of attitudes, towards himself and others, is no more than that which exists within his own mind. Phase I keeps him in Karma, but Phase II and III show him the road home.

RETROGRADE VENUS
IN TAURUS

Here the individual is most comfortable during Phase III of the Retrograde Process where he can immerse himself in all he feels he has acquired in the past. He is constantly identifying his sense of security and feelings of self-worth with what he has accomplished or gathered unto himself unconsciously from prior incarnations as well as every moment before the present.

In some cases this individual is Karmically tied to a love in a past life that has never been fully realized. As a result, quantity or quality of love in this life never really seems to be enough to fill the empty space left by such a past relationship. He is used to feelings of absolute security and will not settle for a love in this life which offers less.

In his younger years he tends to be shy, and throughout life he withdraws into himself while silently pleading with others to pull him out. He wants to be reached and touched, but he does not want to admit it. He tries quietly to draw others into him while at the same time he is afraid of them. His greatest problem centers around his tendency to crystallize certain feelings early in life, and as the years and circumstances of experiences fly by, he sits in his congestion of past feelings, trying desperately to reapply them to each new situation. When this doesn't work he starts unconsciously believing that at least part of the world is passing him by.

His expectations of the opposite sex are usually unrealistic, owing to the powerful self-delusions he has been holding for many years. If any individual can silently collect one chip on his shoulder after another, until he is actually carrying an invisible tree, it would be the person with Retrograde Venus in Taurus.

RETROGRADE VENUS IN GEMINI

Here the individual spends a great deal of time trying to learn what others think of him. Often he changes his likes and dislikes to align with whomever he is with at the moment. He does this because he needs feedback from people in order to understand those parts of himself he thinks he likes. As a result, his life becomes more acceptance-oriented than goal-oriented.

Because of the mutable qualities of Gemini this Retrograde can function during all three phases, but here Venus never fully acquires the personal richness it is trying to establish. Instead, all occurs on thought levels where the individual's love nature ultimately becomes based on ideas and concepts rather than personal feelings. It is important to understand that since the love nature is constantly reidentifying itself because of thoughts received from others, this individual is less personal with himself than most other people. He tends to focus much of his life on the ideas of others which he understands the least. As a result, his relationships tend to confuse him.

Experiencing difficulties with the opposite sex, he looks for reasons within himself to explain the uneasiness he feels in their presence. The problem is that the mental part of him (Gemini) has dualistic masculine qualities, while the feeling part of him (Retrograde Venus) has innately stubborn feminine qualities. The blending of these creates a cross vibration resulting in unsureness when he is confronted with sexual situations. All humans are partly male and partly female, but during the formative years of childhood the changeable qualities of Gemini, influenced by the Retrograde effect, make it difficult for the individual to establish a strong sexual identity that he can firmly believe in. As he grows older, however, and relives some of his childhood concepts, he begins to change his thought constructions into new understandings of his place in humanity. Ultimately he sees love as not sexual at all, but rather as a universal acceptance of his kinship with mankind. To reach this, he must overcome a past life Karma in which he underwent difficulties in identifying the male and female parts of himself. In the current life he unconsciously tries to satisfy both until he realizes that his identity is based on neither one, but rather on the interplay of positive and negative energies which when blended are the source of all creative thought.

RETROGRADE VENUS
IN CANCER

Here the individual is most comfortable in Phase III where he constantly relives his early childhood role relationships with his parents. In the male this can amount to a strong "Oedipus Complex" in which he has never really understood his love for his mother. The counterpart also exists in the female as the "Electra Complex." In either case, the individual keeps asserting that he wants to be on his own, but underneath it all he really doesn't know how to let go of the protective feelings he needed in his childhood.

Living through a dependency Karma, every step into his future brings him closer and closer to the womb he never wanted to leave. He reconstructs his life with people who represent all the early childhood conflicts that he doesn't know how to release. One of his greatest problems is that he tends to construct feeling and reactions to people based upon past memories of who they remind him of. Unfortunately, he traps himself into more Karma each time he does this.

In marriage he projects early feelings towards his parents onto his spouse. In some cases he will even marry an individual that reminds him of his parent of the opposite sex. Basing too much of his opinion of himself on what elders think of him, he must learn to work on developing his own estimation of his self worth.

All of his feelings are based on seeing the world through a "family-like" structure. This gives a shell of protection from within which he can peek out at all he sees around him. Interestingly enough, he also complains that this shell keeps him from experiencing all that he would like to. Still,his greatest strength comes later in life when it becomes important for him to give to his own children and grandchildren all the security and comfort around which his values have been built.

RETROGRADE VENUS
IN LEO

Here the individual is most comfortable during Phase I of the Retrograde Process. Having an unusually strong power complex, he projects himself into all he does. When inspired, he can give much strength to others, but he is not always sure of their sincerity, and has a tendency to silently judge them.

Sometimes he tests others to see if they are worthy of his company. As a result, he tends to place more burdens upon himself than he actually needs. But, at the same time, these artificial burdens increase his feelings of self-esteem. Playing the role of martyr, he can convince himself that he has a cross to bear in terms of giving love that is unappreciated.

His greatest problem is that he wants to be overbearing and outgoing, but the Retrograde vibration does not always produce in others the effects he is trying too hard to achieve. During Phase I, he can actually frighten others by the power of his straightforwardness, then sensing the negative reaction he has caused, he pulls himself away from the very individuals he wants to be close to rather than admitting that it was he himself who overreacted. This Venus position is less detrimental to the individual than it is to those who want sincerely to relate closely to him, and find it difficult.

He brings with him into this life a Karma that involves him with constant display. And, the more he becomes the object of display, the less he is able to experience the richness of interaction with others on an equal basis.

RETROGRADE VENUS IN VIRGO

This is one of the most difficult positions for Retrograde Venus for here the individual brings with him into this life a powerfully high ideal of what love should be. As a result he never quite experiences this in people he relates to as each one falls short of his expectancy. He unconsciously judges the imperfections he feels and sees in others. As a result, he not only becomes reluctant to experience love, but when he is fortunate enough to feel love, he keeps picking it apart until the feelings become merely a collection of analytical theories.

He stays in Phase III most, where he is introverted for fear of being hurt by others. Actually, this individual is experiencing the Karma of being forced to understand human frailty inasmuch as love's perfection, while an ideal that we all aspire to, should not be expected as a reality in the human condition. It is during this third phase that the individual questions why none of his past relationships were fulfilling his needs. And, it is exactly this framework of thought — "to make love work" — which keeps the individual from ever really finding out what the experience of love really is. The Retrograde action of the planet not only leaves him judging others' imperfections, but as he directs the energy inward he tends to transfer this Karma to himself. As a result, he constantly finds himself lacking in terms of what he should be in the eyes of others.

He must learn to see himself clearly and learn to like himself, not in terms of all of the ideals he has crystallized in his mind, but in the proper perspective of the reality of the world within which he lives.

RETROGRADE VENUS IN LIBRA

Here, the ruling Venus finds itself more at home than in any other position. As the individual is swayed from one Retrograde Phase to another by the different individuals in his life, he comes to feel more needed. His concept of love is highly romantic and is dependent more on ideas or things which people represent than the fulfilling of his own physical tastes and needs. Some with this position experiment with homosexuality as the love need tries to rise out of the conventionality of society's tradition. There is usually an unconscious contrariness which manifests in nearly all the individual does. He will give, providing no one asked, and he will serve, if no one required, and he will be most obedient providing no one demanded. He responds poorly to force, pressure or the demands of others.

His natural identity is to quietly seek out the needs of others, and in some fashion be useful enough to fulfill them. On a very deep level he is not at all sure of what he really wants for himself. He is in a constant state of change, trying to tune himself to whatever seems fulfilling to others. Highly aware of the psychological games society plays he can in fact be one of the most skillful players. He will convince himself that certain people cannot live without him when in fact this is a projection of his own need in reverse.

He can be happy by fulfilling himself with nearly anyone who suits his unconscious tastes, because truly he never relates to others, but merely divides himself in two — and then using the other individual as a mirror to the part of him he wants to identify with at the moment, winds up making friends with, talking to, and yes, even making love to himself!

His Karma is rooted in the balancing of his value systems through relationships, and only when he is sure of this, will he settle down and truly stand for the idea he loves the most.

RETROGRADE VENUS IN SCORPIO

This is a very difficult position for Retrograde Venus as the Scorpio drive keeps pushing the individual past his own contentment. He never feels fulfilled, but rather that all he is seeking is just around the next corner or buried in the next well in his mind. Spending much time in Phase I he seeks future gratification, but unfortunately he keeps thinking that he will find his ideal in another person, place, or situation rather than at the deepest recesses of his own being. He is intense and secretive about his love nature and at the same time keenly interested in the private feelings of others. As such, for all he sees in others, he has difficulty experiencing what he is looking for in himself.

He goes through long periods in which he is sure that his discontent is sexual but it goes much deeper than that. The truth is that in past incarnations he went through experiences which caused him not to like himself on unconscious levels. He feels alienated from the ideals he senses within him. And, for all he may try, he seems unable to convince himself of his own self-worth.

As this pattern continues, he is prone to behavior which only reinforces inner feelings of failure and separates him further from all that he truly wants. In some instances, the root of the problem may well be a past-life love that he depended on and by which he was ultimately disillusioned. Where this is the case, there is usually a repeat of the same experience early in this life.

He has difficulty feeling completely at ease with the opposite sex, and until he confronts himself can invent many reasons for this. Still, he does not allow himself to become vulnerable to others on his deepest levels for he has been hurt in the past.

To learn to forgive is important for those with this Venus position, but the individual should understand that forgiveness is not possible without forgetting. With this placement, the individual can function during all three Retrograde Phases, but his greatest evolution comes during Phase III where through a re-evaluation of all he has lived through he can transcend the feelings of lower Karmic levels in his past.

RETROGRADE VENUS IN SAGITTARIUS

This is a very lonely position for the Retrograde Venus. The individual values his freedom more than the personal intimacy that Venus promises. Phase I of the Retrograde Process is emphasized so that he keeps projecting himself from one rainbow to another, never staying long enough in any one place to allow Venus to absorb the full vibration of his environment. He doesn't readily take advice from others. Of all the Zodiac placements, he experiences the most and at the same time feels he is still missing out on something.

This is also a difficult placement for marriage, and is often the cause for divorce due to an overly restless nature. There is difficulty fulfilling all the individual feels he needs, and as a result he is often confusing to others. He sees the world as a giant smorgasbord with untold numbers of offerings to be tasted, and never likes to get involved in anything too deeply. The quantity of life experience becomes more important than the quality. And as his higher mind roams the far reaches of the universe looking for a place it can feel at home, he tends to ignore each bird in the hand seeking two more in the bush.

His ideals coming from prior lifetimes are high, and although he may not always live up to them, he keeps searching for people, places and circumstances which makes him feel more close to these past idealistic experiences. He usually has a good sense of self worth and a fairly strong ego, which he keeps healthy by immersing himself in most of what life has to offer. Although this position is difficult for lasting intimate relationships, it does give the individual an extremely colorful scope of life experiences. In past incarnations he learned how to develop a natural feel for the world around him, which he now depends on for his knowledge much more than the words of books or teachers.

RETROGRADE VENUS
IN CAPRICORN

In this position, Venus usually indicates marriage to an older partner or an individual symbolizing authority from the past. Sometimes the spouse resembles the restrictions imposed during childhood and in other cases it brings forward the restrictions imposed on the individual in a former life.

The most comfortable period is during Phase III where prior times which represented safety and security are repeated, as the individual keeps seeking to re-experience protective relationships. In many ways, he is a collector; be it antiques, or memorabilia from a former time in history, or even people, it always symbolizes his need to bring something to what he feels is a necessary completion.

His life is filled with bannisters, shapes, and forms, for all he feels, he desires to crystallize within himself in order to fulfill the sense of security he is trying to establish. He can seem mature for his age during his youth, but all the while he is inwardly rebelling at all the restrictions he feels on his freedom. He is retentive of thoughts, ideas, and feelings (including the negative ones) for many years, and tends to deny himself pleasure or happiness during the first half of life in the hope of some greater promise at another time. As he grows older, however, he comes to realize how much he has tried to recreate his past, and how much that has bound him. Then he changes radically and starts to make his outlook more practical in terms of his own needs. All the while, he feels out of tune with people at or near his own age. In essence, he lives his life backwards, experiencing the burdens of old age in his youth and the freedom of his teenage years, during his old age.

This is one of the horoscope indicators of family Karma. Usually, there is such an imbalance coming from a past incarnation, and repeated during the early years of this life, that the individual spends most of his time running from himself, then, about half-way through life when he realizes this, he tries to make up for all he knows he missed.

RETROGRADE VENUS IN AQUARIUS

Here the individual is most comfortable during Phase I of the Retrograde Process where he can explore the needs he feels glimpses of, before they are actually real in his life. At times he can be overbearing in his desire to help others to the point that he can actually hinder them without meaning to. He is highly independent and cannot easily accept restrictions or limitations on his life. He will at times, scatter his affections among so many things, people, and experiences, that individuals close to him will feel thwarted in their own abilities to focus their energies. Most of his scattering, however, is merely a reflection of his highly changeable nature. He is usually overly sensitive to his environment and must keep shifting his approach to life in order to feel balanced.

He can be a rebel, and likes his freedom. He is too sensitive to people imposing their will on him. But, at the same time, he does feel that he knows what's best for others. Thus, there tends to be a lack of perspective in his personal relationships.

He has an avid interest in nearly everything, and tends to get involved with some of the strangest people. All that is conventional is too boring to focus any great length of attention on, yet he needs to feel secure. He is actually much less sure of himself than he would want others to know.

During Phase I he actively explores the unknown, while during Phase III he re-explores unknown or little used bits of knowledge from the past. It is during this third phase that many with this position enjoy exploring ancient civilizations or little-known documents from other periods in history. In many this brings a great interest in Astrology and Esoteric subjects. With all the artificialities of life stripped away, this is a very lonely person. His impersonal need to help others is really a disguise for his trying to earn his way back into a humanity that has in another incarnation somehow rejected him. Thus, he never fully expects total intimacy for any great period of time, but is contented just to know that his beliefs and ideas are now being accepted. And, he will go miles out of his way just to earn this acceptance.

RETROGRADE VENUS IN PISCES

Here the individual spends most of his time in Phase III of the Retrograde Process as he keeps reabsorbing the dream of love gone past. He experiences a great deal of loneliness and feels silently that he is separated from the tangible reality he thinks he wants. Highly romantic in past incarnations, he keeps pulling himself back into past fantasies. He is unconventional, and likes to think of himself as being independent as long as he has someone to lean on. Being highly impressionable as a youth, much of what he lives through are re-enactments of the fairy tales he identified with as a child. It is usually not until mid-life that he actually begins to see this.

He is a hard person to reach because he is actually possessive of the illusions which prevent him from seeing himself, and everytime his looking glass is about to be shattered he re-creates new extensions to those fantasies in order to free himself as much as possible from the restrictions he feels in his present reality. He does not truly feel that he is comfortable in the circumstances that surround him in this incarnation. Yet, he does not realize that he picked them himself. Nor does he want to realize this. He finds it easier to believe that life has been sweeping him along, at time even against his own will. He has a great fear of being owned by either people or circumstances which might at some time in the future put demands on him. In his unconscious insecurity he feels he might possibly not be able to meet these demands. Thus, he gives himself more cause for escaping his true inner feelings.

This placement of Venus tends towards masochism which creates many situations which punish the cosmic self and at the same time create greater sorrow in the lower personal self. The more this person allows past illusions to enter into his present feelings, the more he separates from any feelings of the present that he says he want to experience. In relationships with others, he tends to retreat into the dull Piscean cloud of mist that he surrounds himself with as a buffer against the present.

This is one of the most difficult positions for the realization of personal love. As such he must work through the Karma of lifting his expectations off of the personal plane of expectancy for the lower self, and in its place begin to experience a Divine attunement upon which he can base his reality.

Many individuals with this placement have experienced losing personal love in a past incarnation. Now, in this life they unconsciously keep looking for aspects of this love in every person they meet, until the day they realize that their Soul has chosen to be transformed beyond the needs of selfish gratification. As a result, the sorrow in this placement is found during Phase III of the Retrograde Process, which changes into an active giving to humanity when the individual impersonally switches into Phase I.

RETROGRADE VENUS IN THE FIRST HOUSE

This individual needs much attention and yet never quite fully feels fulfilled. He is preoccupied with how he appears to others. There is much egocentricity as feelings of self-love run much higher on the conscious than on the unconscious level. Underneath his constant seeking for more attention he has much ambivalence about himself. Though he thinks of himself as a creature of love, he tends not to understand just how much love to give out to others. He either gives too much or not enough. In general the amount of love he experiences in either giving or receiving is inappropriate to the situation.

He likes others to let him live his own life, yet he can become overly possessive of others for fear of being left alone. This conflict can cause many problems in areas of relationships as well as marriage.

In his love experiences, he goes through the threefold Retrograde Process which keeps emphasizing the positive or negative nature more according to which phase of the pattern he is in, than whether circumstances in his relationships with others warrant his responses. He is not necessarily a great giver of love, but he can absorb much love from others. He needs this for his self-confidence.

This placement is most difficult during Phase II of the Retrograde Process because the need for harmony combined with the First House expression of unity within oneself cannot tolerate a cross vibration for any great period of time. He is most at home during Phase I where expectation runs at its highest. Even in this phase as he tries to emphasize his Venus positively to move him into the future he still experiences the naturally negative magnetic quality of Venus through which he is expecting to be the receiver of love. The greatest key towards happiness in this position is based on realistic self-acceptance.

RETROGRADE VENUS
IN THE SECOND HOUSE

Here the individual is most comfortable during Phase III, where the naturally absorbing rays of Venus try to recreate past experiences which offer the individual feelings of security. He is unusually possessive of all past value systems which worked for him. He likes to absorb the universe around him as it again offers the security he was so used to feeling. He can be highly materialistic, while seeking to reestablish and strengthen all past feelings of self-worth. Having a strong tendency to repeat all things which he likes he becomes a creature of many habits. So great is his need for assurance on the plane of physical and material substance, that it is difficult for him to be overly generous without feeling that he is losing something in the process.

With this placement, the individual tries to internalize all he values in the universe. In many cases this increases the usual possessiveness of the Second House.

With all his security needs, he is not powerfully competitive, for there is a certain amount of laziness inherent here. The individual will experience difficulties with the opposite sex as a result of his own possessiveness or fear of being possessed. He is frugal with affections, while at the same time tending to inwardly exaggerate his feelings. He likes to do things his own way. He can become angry when he feels others are impinging on his methods of doing things.

Many with this position can become great artisans, but always it will be building something from the past. If ever an individual decided to earn his living by building graceful chariots in the twenty-first century, it would be the person with Venus Retrograde in the Second House.

Here the individual is experiencing a Karma of attachment to past life love and comfort in terms of people, objects, and circumstances. He bases all security on the continuity of form and substance in the current life.

RETROGRADE VENUS
IN THE THIRD HOUSE

This is a very difficult position for Venus, for the unpredictability of Gemini is constantly throwing the individual from one Retrograde Phase to the other. He seems to be out of synchronization in most of his relationships. He either loves too much or too little in relation to love received from the other individual. Or, his love becomes out of tune in the time dimension, such that he can experience great love for an individual while he is preparing to be with them, be in a rather low keyed vibration during actual personal contact, and then experience the greatest part of love after he is no longer with the person by looking back and recreating them in his mind.

Thus, the individual in his love life, and his relationships with others experiences great problems in trying to live in the here and now. Forces outside of himself constantly act on this Retrograde Venus, creating conditions that he feels he is either not yet ready for, or already passed. And, as he moves through these conditions in his life, he keeps trying to tune his feelings under the domain of his mental plane activities. As a result, he spends much time

analyzing all that he feels. This is a poor position for marriage, as the mutable qualities of the Third House keep
throwing the individual out of mental tune with his own
feelings. In areas of expression, the individual tends not
always to mean what he says, but to be more interested in the
feeling it creates in the listener. He is basically insecure,
especially with people his own age. Very often, in order to
feel accepted, he will say or do things that he knows are not
himself, but which would gain the social acceptance that he
is craving.

His Karma is with people's feelings, as he keeps trying
to find the ways in which he can satisfy others as well as
himself. There is a good amount of Karmic loneliness inherent in his Venus position, for this is the individual that can
feel alone in a crowd.

RETROGRADE VENUS
IN THE FOURTH HOUSE

Venus is well placed in the Fourth House enjoying a
good degree of comfort during all three Retrograde Phases.
While the latter two phases may cause the individual to be
somewhat introverted, this does not make him too uncomfortable. He likes to have a person of the opposite sex to lean
on, for his concept of love always involves a degree of paren-
tal protectiveness, which although he may resent outwardly, he greatly needs inwardly.

He is childlike, continually recreating the kind of love
he experienced in his earlier years. The individual has never
fully outgrown his love and attachment of the parent of the
opposite sex. Thus, he keeps trying to draw himself back
into the womb. Sometimes he experiences fear of people and
as a result he has more difficulty expressing his likes to the
outside world than to those close to him who he knows for a
long period of time. He has difficulty understanding stran-
gers, for in terms of love he sees his world as one giant
family — his own! Often, he feels he is obliged to relate to
others in the outside world as if they actually were his own
family. This is done unconsciously, but it puts burdens on
him in terms of limiting the number of individuals and outside situations in which he can feel comfortable.

He is working through a Karma which keeps repeating the beginnings of the experiences of love until he has enough confidence to actually believe that through it he has the security he needs to be able to express it to the outside world.

RETROGRADE VENUS IN THE FIFTH HOUSE

Here the individual is most comfortable during Phase I of the Retrograde Process. He usually has a very strong ego which expresses itself through the creative process. As a result, he can sometimes overwhelm people by the amount of inner confidence he seems to have. This is not actually the case as the combination of the planet and house tend to produce a great deal of acting in the presence of others so that the individual can live with his own self-consciousness. He tends to project his feelings into others because he cannot tolerate rejection. Yet, he can reject others just before he senses they will reject him by rationalizing that they don't measure up to his standards.

In some instances he is carrying with him an inner self-pride which others must reinforce before he allows them into his circle. He will go out of his way to maintain what he feels is his self-respect and he can often deny himself the full enjoyment of life by trying to live up to an image that he has created for himself.

He feels best when he is able to help others who he sees as less capable than himself. Thus, some with this placement may get a great deal of pleasure by teaching retarded children or other handicapped individuals to be more self-expressive.

One of the greatest difficulties in this position of Venus is that the individual constantly frustrates himself adhering to expectations which are unrealistically too high. He is unable to find the perfect person who can fulfill all he thinks he needs. Thus, in the most basic way, he is working on the Karmic lesson of contentment. He can make much inner growth by realizing that his life is less dependent on other people than he believes. The dissatisfaction he feels in others is always the dissatisfaction he has created in himself. When he learns to expect less from life, he will realize the joy he is looking for.

RETROGRADE VENUS
IN THE SIXTH HOUSE

This is a very shaky placement for sensitive Venus as the individual always pressures himself through the sense of obligation he feels. There is a tendency to experience disappointing relationships, particularly in areas associated with work. While all three Phases are difficult the individual feels safer in the Third Phase where he withdraws into himself, holds back his feelings, and tries to rationalize all he is with all he thinks he must be to others. This creates an inner sorrow which prevents him from functioning at his best. He has to guard against allowing his feelings to go to extremes, as he unconsciously believes that the world is a contaminated disorderly place.

He backs away from others as he doesn't quite understand how to handle the imperfections he sees in them. One of his biggest problems is that he can allow his feelings to become computerized. He does this by pre-programming his relationships so that he can figure out how they will work in advance. Thus his approach to people is very mechanical and every thought and action he receives from another is seen as part of the many moves in his planned chess game of life.

He can do many favors for others but he is only contented when he knows they can be returned. Unfortunately he has a tendency to judge others by what they do, measuring their deeds and actions against his ideals. Thus, he lives a double standard, not fully realizing that the ideals of all the people he knows may well be as high as his own and that their inability to live up to them in his presence is a reflection of his own human frailties.

He uses most of his energy in sublimating and repressing many of his needs. From this limited vantage point, he deals with his Karma of trying to create perfection in his environment. He has to learn that the world is already perfect and that he cannot improve on it. Somewhere between his perfect idealism and the unrecognized needs he has for others is the balance that will bring him happiness.

RETROGRADE VENUS
IN THE SEVENTH HOUSE

This is one of the most unique positions for Venus Retrograde. As ruler of the Seventh House it can be very beneficial if the individual uses it to see a true reflection of himself through the eyes of those he loves. However, if he fights the fact that many of his ideas, thoughts, and feelings seem to be rejected and does not understand the reasons why, then he can actually cause an imbalance in the entire horoscope.

His moods and feelings are swayed by the world around him; there is no boundary between the feelings that come from within himself and the feelings that he internalizes from others.

As he glides from one Retrograde Phase to another he assumes different identities all of which are directed at the self but none of which are truly his center. He is unusually conscious of how he can actually be turned inside out, losing his spontaniety in the desire to be thought better of by others. As such, he is an extremist. In the course of a single day he can shift gears entirely into a very purposeful desire to displease others. His feelings are like a pendulum swinging from side to side by the winds of other people's feelings; always passing the center but rarely staying there. He is never quite sure of whether or not he is seen as being proper in the eyes of others.

Highly sensitive to his external environment, he first bends with it, losing himself in it and then runs from it to recover. Still he doesn't like to do things alone and this causes him to experience the frustration of wanting to know himself and yet not wanting to have to fully separate himself from others. He is living out a Karma of experiencing the imbalanced parts of himself through the ways in which others see him.

RETROGRADE VENUS
IN THE EIGHTH HOUSE

Here the individual spends a great deal of time in Phase I of the Retrograde Process where the desire nature powers the need to create future fulfillment now. He feels a great deal of internal intensity which he does not release easily.

The emotion of love is often coupled with past anger and resentment directed at some individual or experience which caused painful memories.

He is highly perceptive but does not like others to see into him. His ideals are also very high, but if the individual is unable to realize his dream in real life his actions can run in the opposite direction.

Sexually he vascillates from periods of intense need to periods of total lack of interest. His sexual drive is related to a strong desire to possess. At times he can be secretly jealous of others who seem to have more than he does.

He has a tendency to hide from his own feelings, not wanting to face the wall he puts up between his outer and inner life. There is a great deal of impatience with this placement, as the individual is not only experiencing the depth of his own needs but also is feeling the influences of other people's needs. This often brings a conflict between the manner in which he relates to society and the way he truly feels. Often there is a great deal of resentment in this position of Venus as the individual feels cheated or deprived of much that he believes is rightfully his.

He tends to go through life doing things the hard way, envious of how others can reach the same goals with less effort.

This position experiences a feeling of isolation from the world. There is past-life residue of lost love. As a result, the individual finds it difficult to fully trust the people he meets in the current life because he unconsciously sees in each one of the symbolic parts of love he was deprived of in the past.

RETROGRADE VENUS
IN THE NINTH HOUSE

Here the individual experiences a great need for personal freedom. He does not allow others to hamper or impede his space. In some people this position manifests in a great love for a spiritual life.

Isolated from the intense subjective qualities of social relationships he seeks peace within himself through his ability to stay out of the thick of things. This may manifest as the desire for the seclusion of a monestary, a mountain spring or walking barefoot through the woods.

There is a great need here for a sense of the largeness of life and the individual often sacrifices closeness with other people in order to fulfill this need. He is highly independent and does not like to be put into the mold of other people's wishes. At the same time, this is a very difficult position for marriage or any other relationship of a lasting nature, for here in the Ninth House the personal qualities of Venus are transferred into a more cosmic reality. Thus the individual's sense of self-identity has a different quality than that of most other people he meets. Because of the way he sees the ebb and flow of the universal tide of life he does not like to make permanent commitments.

Many of the things he does he will do alone and he will go through numerous experiences with many different people, most of whom seem to represent philosophies which are quite foreign to the ideas he was raised with.

He tends to be difficult to understand as he is not ordinarily motivated by the ideas which prompt his contemporaries.

This is the one person who can actually achieve a rare degree of peace amidst a world of chaos. At the same time, he cannot easily transmit this to others. In some instances he can be artistically talented as a result of a past incarnation.

Whatever the life style is like, he will experience some degree of conflict between feeling that he should be involved in society's needs, and knowing that there is as much reason for him not to do so.

Karmically he marches to the beat of a different drummer, and brings with him into this life a very strong residue of doing what he likes to do when he likes to do it. He is easy to get along with but impossible to own, for his ingrained instinct is basically to be a free spirit.

RETROGRADE VENUS IN THE TENTH HOUSE

Here the individual spends much of his time in Phase

III of the Retrograde Process. He likes to look backward over the accomplishments of his life's desires and needs to know that he is accepted by those he has previously looked up to as being superior to himself. He wants social acceptance but does not like to seek it. Thus his outward expression of creativity is hampered by whether or not he expects others to reject him. He can become overly conscious of how he is integrating with others and as a result becomes highly sensitive in social situations.

Capable of internalizing the feelings of others he often feels responsible for fulfilling the needs of those around him. This tends to make him less than comfortable when in public circumstances. He tends to be self-conscious, and sometimes backs away from the directions he wants to move in the most.

He feels heavily the responsibility from the past which he is not sure he is able to live up to. In the horoscope of a male this can cause difficulty with females as a result of being under the dominion of an older female early in life.

Usually there is a great deal of creative ability already developed in past incarnations, but the individual must develop confidence in himself now if he is to express it.

Karmically he goes through life trying to collect the feelings which will give him the sense of purpose that he needs. As soon as he can do this he will begin to express the meaning in his life that he has been looking for.

RETROGRADE VENUS
IN THE ELEVENTH HOUSE

This is one of the most difficult positions for the Retrograde Venus, as it distracts from the creative process. The individual rarely experiences a feeling of being settled. The patient qualities of Venus are disturbed by an ever-present drifting curiosity during the First Phase of the Retrograde Process. He is reaching for fulfillment in many different directions at the same time. Sometimes, the sense of reality is so unique that the individual is almost totally detached from his earth plane identity. He wants to taste everything, but he doesn't know why. At times he becomes highly possessive of thought itself, to the point that the unfair greed he sees in others on the material plane is a reflection of what he himself is doing mentally. He must truly learn to discriminate, for while each new whim and fancy that attracts is beautiful in and of itself, the blending of all of these is often more inharmonious than he can feel comfortable with.

He expresses a great deal of personal rejection which ultimately makes him become more detached. Exploring the many realms and possibilities of thought that exist in the universe he does not always know how to blend them together in his personal life. Still, he can be more of a help to others than he can to himself.

One of his biggest difficulties is that his secret desire to go through his experiences by himself keeps him slightly apart from the rest of humanity that he loves so dearly. Some with this position go through bizarre sexual experiences as the need for exploration is always trying to transcend society's norms.

In past incarnations he has experienced so many different things that appealed to him that he has become a constant seeker for that which he has not yet experienced. His dreams can be unrealistic but the nature of his personal reality is such that he is totally uninhibited by the restrictions of conventional society. His future is entirely based upon how much he clings to his past fantasies.

RETROGRADE VENUS
IN THE TWELFTH HOUSE

Here the individual stays in Phase III of the Retrograde Process where he does not openly express feelings that he thinks might be rejected. In many instances there is an attachment to a past life love that has not yet been broken, and as the individual lives each day of his future he keeps trying to recreate his past. He can be happy when he is alone but does not like to feel abandoned by others. At the slightest hint of rejection he can go into long periods of feeling sorry for himself, for he almost instinctively knows that he came into this incarnation leaving his true love behind. As such, he tries to content himself by finding symbolic aspects of that love in all the people he meets, but underneath all of his emotional energy he is still holding onto romantic concepts of a time gone by. Thus, he finds it difficult to be fully gratified by his current life experiences as all he perceives is seen through the colored glasses of his preconceived concepts.

He walks through life with a silent hurt and doesn't like others to make demands on him. Usually there is a great deal of bottled up emotion in this position, and while others rarely see it, the individual is almost constantly aware of this part of him which keeps refusing to come into the current life.

He can be highly creative if he is not forced, for he tends to spend a great deal of time dwelling within himself, when he can actually gain his strength but unconsciously reabsorbing past memories of moments when he truly was at peace with himself.

He is not a seeker of outward popularity as much as inner fulfillment. Sometimes there can be clandestine love affairs with this position, through which the individual tries to sustain the illusion in the present of what was once a reality in his past. Emotionally timed, he tends to allow much of life's opportunities to pass him by. He will reach happiness when he realizes that he is not really losing his past by living in the present.

RETROGRADE MARS
ESOTERIC SYMBOL

Mars the planet of vitality, energy, sexuality and the desire for expression is symbolized by (♂ or ♂) the Cross of Matter angularly placed over the Circle of Spirit. In modern symbology the Cross appears as an arrow, thus indicating the Martian nature of thrusting forward. But it is of interest to note that the cross or arrow is always slanted, showing an imbalance as well as incompleteness in this symbol. Thus, it thrusts outward away from itself as the cross or arrow accelerates away from the Circle of Spirit to find completeness in eternal things or other people.

This is the only personal planet in which the Cross of Matter is placed above the Circle of Spirit. Thus, the need for carnal, material and physical fulfillment takes precedence here over the Spirit and can in fact fulfill the Spirit.

When Mars is Retrograde, the symbol's meaning becomes inverted and the individual refuses to accept the fulfillment of his Spirit, by his achievements and conquests in the material or physical part of his life.

From past incarnations he has learned to sublimate, twist, deny, distort or negate the fulfillment of his physical needs unless the needs of his Spirit are met first.

It is interesting to note that because the Cross of Matter is angular even when this symbol is inverted, it still represents an imbalance. In fact, probably more so as the arrow-cross of desire for fulfillment in matter is not only pointing backwards to the past but also now provides less stability for the Circle of Spirit to rest on. It is almost as if the Circle of Spirit is trying to meet the present while dragging as a weight under and behind it the physical desires from the past.

RETROGRADE MARS
PERSONALITY

This individual experiences a lack of contact with the pure reality of his needs systems. Thus he goes through difficulties in coordinating thought and action. The past of his life which he actually lives through is at least slightly removed from his consciousness. He also expereinces sexual difficulties due to the reverse magnetism of the Retrograde Planet. This is mostly due to his inability to regulate the flow of energy which this placement causes him to experience.

Much that he will live through depends less on thought or emotions than his ability to handle his own energy levels in coordination with those energies he receives from others. He can react very strongly to a person and develop a very powerful feeling in a positive or negative sense based purely on the energy level he is receiving rather than for the human reasons he attaches to his reactions.

Because of this, the individual's relationships are nearly always distorted and on the sexual level seem to symbolize more of a struggle for survival rather than an actual union with another person.

He can jump to conclusions while at the same time delaying the necessary actions which would correct all that bothers him. If the Retrograde Mars is in an air sign, he is unusually mentally active and it is difficult,for him to learn how to relax.

This Mars position is more difficult for a female than it is for a male because the drive system can be disproportionate to the rest of the horoscope and tends to decrease her femininity. There are very few females with this placement who on the unconscious level have any love for men at all. However, on the conscious level, the apparent opposite is sometimes manifested by putting males on pedestals, creating a type of idol worship which brings the individual closer to her unconscious reality by internally creating the need to pull the pedestal away.

In most placements, Mars Retrograde causes feelings of guilt and blame which isolate the individual, setting him apart from the free flowing interchange of personal relationships that people with Mars direct experience.

RETROGRADE MARS
KARMA

When Mars is Retrograde in the horoscope, all the actions of the individual in the current life are recreations of the past.

The individual tries to find people in this life who symbolize all those who fulfilled him in past incarnations. In his mind he throws them into the roles of these no longer existent figures. With them he tries to act out all that he could not previously express. He tends to over-react in an attempt to forcibly move them into the imaginary roles he has conceived for them. Thus he comes on too strong and sensing rejection but not understanding why, he pulls back into himself never fully experiencing his current life relations in the present moment.

He tends to center on a time from his past which represented a force he had to deal with. Now he unconsciously vibrates to that exact same force, be it anger, revenge, hostility, or misdirected action in every person in the present. In some cases he may be carrying a former life grudge which makes him mistrust other people's actions. In at least one past life he has lived through suspicious or deceptive actions on the part of others. The residue of this in the current life weigh heavily on the present behavior.

RETROGRADE MARS
IN ARIES

Here the Retrograde Mars is most comfortable in Phase I where the impulsive qualities of Aries combine with the Martian thrust to try to forcibly create the future before any external force brings it about. There is so much residue of past life insecurity that the individual finds it very difficult to live through Phase III where he would have to evaluate his past actions and take full stock of himself. He is still trying to begin what he had started before this life.

He is primitive, highly subjective and can actually live

for many years oblivious to the world around him. He sees only visions he creates and is nearly always sexually unfulfilled. In most instances he tends to fall into the mental trap of over-expectancy. As a result, during those moments when he is moving through Phase II, he feels a great deal of boredom living out that which is not really new to him. His general discontent with himself makes it difficult for him to reflect well through others. He thinks he knows what he wants but an objective general overview of his life indicates that he is not usually in touch with himself long enough to understand his true inner desires. The beauty of this placement is that as he goes through life, the Retrograde action of the planet keeps thrusting him back into himself so that ultimately he comes to understand that his desires never were the symbols he sought in the outer world, but rather a much deeper inner desire to establish within himself the essence of self-esteem.

This is a very difficult position for marriage, as the individual is overly self-conscious. He needs to develop more sensitivity to others. Too often, he sees others as competitiors in the arena of his own growth, rather than as separate individuals with needs and feelings which may well be as intense as his own.

He can achieve much once he measures himself against himself rather than against other people or outside forces beyond his control.

RETROGRADE MARS IN TAURUS

In Taurus, Mars is most comfortable during Phase III where the individual reabsorbs his past thereby giving him the security he is looking for. He is basically afraid of taking new actions. As a result he creates his life in terms of his past, feeling more sure that all will go well. Preprogramming of the physical needs is strong. He holds resentment and often mistakingly directs his anger back on himself as punishment. The person wants to feel close to others but holds himself back, creating inner tension instead.

This is particularly frustrating because the Taurean

desire for warmth and closeness is inhibited by the tendency of the Retrograde Mars to linger in the Third Phase which symbolizes introspection.

In many ways, this is the perennnial child unwilling to grow and transform the patterns of his youth. He is a creature of habit, and can retain many bad habits simply because the quantity of experience is able to fulfill the Taurean need for abundance. He likes to spend time alone but wants to know that he is not left alone. Thus, he backs away from advances made towards him while at the same time knowing that he would be miserable if they did not exist.

The Karma of this position relates to the individual's learning how to accept his own social and physical needs. He can actually drain himself by the internalization of his conflicts in these areas.

RETROGRADE MARS
IN GEMINI

Retrograde Mars combines with Gemini's flexibility so that it can function during all three Retrograde Phases. During Phase I the mental curiosity pushes the person into future experiences. He becomes keenly interested in all that he has not yet experienced.

In Phase II he has less exuberance and experiences a degree of disappointment while seeing in reality all he envisioned in his imagination in the first phase. Still he experiences the choices that Gemini likes of expressing outwardly that which he is already sure of, while he is testing that which he has not experienced. It is during this phase that he becomes overly concerned about his actions.

This leads him into Phase III where he constantly repeats himself. Of all the positions of Retrograde Mars this is one of the easiest for the individual to deal with. His life lesson is to learn the appropriate amount of force to use in dealings with others.

Sometimes he causes over reactions in himself during Phase III as the Gemini restlessness causes him anxiety during this typically introspective period.

Sexually he experiences a coldness which sometimes

leads him to judge others, particularly in terms of their motives. His Karma is to learn who he is through how he relates with other people. He changes his approach to life according to the ways that the winds of chance happen to be blowing at any particular time, for he is more interested in how he gets by than in having his life actually stand for any particular principle. Thus, he is less honorable than he is adaptable to whatever life throws his way. Avoiding deep involvements, he tends more towards superficiality than experiencing life on a deep level.

He must learn that the intense desires he sees in others are really his own.*

RETROGRADE MARS IN CANCER

This is a very frustrating position for the Retrograde Mars because the Cardinal quality keeps thrusting the person into Phase I where there is a strong desire for new experiences and yet the emotional sensitivity along with the need for child-like protection keeps bounding the individual back into Phase III where his qualities of introversion tend to make him act out his life more within his emotional self rather than through the world around him.

In some instances, particularly in females, there can be a strong Electra Complex in which repressed infantile sexual feelings towards the father continue to govern most of life's desires. The individual is attracted to people of the opposite sex who are very different in age than themselves.

There is a tendency to try to make others part of one's own family and to desire to close in the outer world around oneself.

Since Cancer has so much to do with the formative years, the naturally absorbing introverting qualities of the Third Phase become enhanced and magnified as every future desire is to try to recreate the secure beginnings of life. The individual reacts very strongly to older people in terms of whether or not he is capable of fulfilling their expectancy.

He can hold desires within himself for many years and

*See p. 26 Retrogrades and Thought Projection.

even when these desires do not fulfill him, he has difficulty in redirecting his energies. He has to learn to get more in touch with his impulses that are surfacing from his unconscious so that he doesn't feel impelled to remake the world into the ways his family life should have been.

In other incarnations his traumatic experiences were during his youth and it is only as he symbolically re-enacts them through role playing with others that he can actually bring the desire part of him into the current life.

RETROGRADE MARS IN LEO

Here the individual can become an island unto himself. The pride of Leo combines with the strength of Mars to produce an internal sense of dominion over other pepople. The individual rarely recognizes his effect on others. He can come on too strong causing others to back away from him in fear as they are confronted with the weaknesses within themselves. The seed with which this occurs during Phase I magnifies the intensity of the reaction. The individual's conception of himself is highly subjective based more upon his present impulse than upon the way others reflect back to him. If any individual could have a strong desire to be fair and yet live selfishly at the same time, this would be him.

Sometimes there is difficulty in raising a male child and the individual can actually impede the progress of the child by expecting too much of him.

This person doesn't take advice. He is defensive because he fears losing the illusion of the position he has set up for himself and thus from time to time creates much friction with others.

His goals are so high that when they are powered through Retrograde Mars he wants to reach complete fulfillment in everything he sees. He must learn how unrealistic these expectations are in his daily life.

He brings with him into this life a strong desire to be in command, thus he keeps setting up competitive situations where in reality they may not even exist. Of all the Martian placements this is one which cannot tolerate losing. Appa-

rently some past life efforts were unrewarded and unfulfilled. Now the individual tries to recapture his past by convincing himself that he does have a good degree of power
over his life and all those he allows to touch it.

RETROGRADE MARS
IN VIRGO

This is one of the more difficult positions of Retrograde
Mars in terms of personal relations. If Mars were not Retrograde the individual would measure all desire in terms of
perfected ideas. The Retrograde changes these feelings to
the point where the individual is forced to live his ideals
rather than only to expect them from others. Thus he judges
himself while trying to maintain his illusions of perfection.
He has inner fears of others and relates easier with objects
than with people. He is highly sensitive and over-reacts to
pressure from those around him.

Many people with this placement defend themselves so
much against the reoccurrance of a past hurt that they purposely close themselves off from developing any real intimacy with others. Often they feel slighted by those they
have tried to please in the past.

It is difficult for this person to relax as the mental
energy is stimulated by the sex drive. Sometimes this causes
a very active interest in sexuality, with very little physical
expression.

The individual has a great need to seek perfection
within himself. In former lifetimes he learned how to discriminate between his different desires and now categori-
cally separates everything into neat little compartments in
his mind. Sensing imperfections in the actions of others, he
can experience extreme mistrust with each new person he
meets. As relationships develop he tries to find that one flaw
in another person's character which will ultimately convince him that his pre-programmed ways of dealing with
that person were justified and correct.

If the person with Retrograde Mars in Virgo would listen to what he is saying or thinking of others he would learn
that the perfection he is seeking starts within himself.

RETROGRADE MARS
IN LIBRA

This is perhaps the most difficult position for Retrograde Mars. Here the individual not only has difficulty identifying his own desires but also takes on the desires of others thinking they are his own. Consequently, he experiences a state of limbo as he feels himself being tossed from one side to the other through the wishes, needs and wants of everyone in his life. He brings with him into this incarnation a continuing Karma of not truly understanding what he wants. In the past he lived for the desires of others. Now he experiences difficulty in finding his own center of being. As a result, the search for self-identification becomes so strong that many with this position are powerfully attracted to members of the same sex through whom they eventually hope to find themselves.

The Retrograde Phase that the individual will spend his time in keeps changing according to the person he is with. Having little sense of self-esteem he tries to inter-relate with the Aries quality of every person he meets.

The frustration that the individual experiences becomes heightened as he tries to harmoniously balance the different drives and desires coming from all the people he knows. Ultimately this creates in him a type of emotional paralysis along with a degree of gullibility towards his external environment.

Karmically he is being forced to know who he is amidst everyone he feels he could be.

RETROGRADE MARS
IN SCORPIO

Since Scorpio is the sign of transformation and Mars the planet that energizes all emotion, this individual experiences a very active inner life. Through all three phases the planet works to the individual's benefit, but the inward turning of the Retrograde along with the constant thrust of Mars never gives the individual a chance to rest. He constantly feels that he is not reaching all he should.

In some instances where the Mars is used physically this can amount to severe gluttony. Even if the individual directs his life on the spiritual path, he finds himself confronted with temptations. He always feels that there are external forces preventing him from reaching his goals. Thus he develops an intense energy inside himself in order to overpower these imaginary enemies to his progress.

In some cases he is out of touch with his own need systems. He can be highly impatient in Phase I, totally bored in Phase II and unsatisfied during Phase III as he tries to culminate the burning drive which never ends.

Often, he is carrying a grudge from another lifetime and even in this incarnation, rather than forgiving those who hurt him, he buries his anger into unconscious levels where he will continue to carry it as part of his basic makeup. As a result, he can become his own worst enemy.

Karmically, he must learn that instead of destroying himself, he should be destroying the parts of his old self that have been keeping him alienated from others.

RETROGRADE MARS IN SAGITTARIUS

Here impulsiveness is at its height as the individual wants to experience the whole world — yesterday. His restlessness goes very deep for he never quite knows the priorities of his needs. This scattering occurs not only in the things he does but also internally, in his own self-identification. He tries to experience the whole world in all of its different colors and flavors within himself.

Sometimes animosity is carried over into the present incarnation which keeps the individual from seeing others in true perspective. Much of his life as well as the ways he sees others has no basis in reality.

He has difficulty pinpointing his desires long enough to know if they are meaningful to him. During Phase I he can seem to be overly extroverted and yet nothing he reaches for represents the fullness of all he is seeking. He tries to justify his motives and likes to believe himself right.

This is an especially poor position for marriage as this

person is so much an individualist, as well as a bit of a dreamer, that he hardly stays in one place long enough for another individual to feel that they are fulfilling him.

Karmically he is seeking to find his place in the world. He needs to know the reason for his existence and he finds parts of that reason through each new place he visits and each new person he meets.

He must learn how to balance the philosophical needs of Sagittarius with the physical thirst for experience of Mars. Ultimately the Retrograde nature turns him inward where he learns to transmute his experiences into what is to become the reason for his existence.

RETROGRADE MARS
IN CAPRICORN

Here the individual spends most of his energies trying to build his own feelings of self-worth. He has a tendency to collect all external thoughts, things and people which will construct a pyramid on which he will ultimately sit.

He experiences conflict between the impulsiveness of youth and the reticence of old age. As a result, he constantly creates life experiences with people whose age is different than his as he tries to gain acceptance through different peer groups. He takes all of his actions seriously and sometimes when he is in the third phase he can even imagine responsibility for the actions of others.

Capricorn being an especially Karmic sign because of the rulership of Saturn, brings the individual to experience the effects of all he causes more than any other zodiacal placement for he ultimately realizes that he is responsible for all of his actions. He wants to be responsible for himself and will take no chances in life where he might be open to rejection or failure.

If these individuals put themselves on a spiritual path there is no limit to what they can achieve for they are their own best guide. Highly purposeful during Phase I of the Retrograde Process, fully functional during Phase II, and deeply introspective during Phase III, these people know exactly where they are going in life as well as how to get there.

RETROGRADE MARS
IN AQUARIUS

Here the individual is most comfortable in Phase I in which he desires to roam where there are no footsteps ahead of him. He puts no limitations to the freedom he wants to experience and he is carrying within him in this incarnation the continuation of a liberated instinct developed in former lives. Once shackled by the boundaries of society, he rebels against current life norms, and will seek new rules which transcend that which already exists.

His life is extremely colorful reflecting an "anything goes" attitude and all that stops him from experiencing the world as a playground are the institutions and traditions that he bumps into. These he quickly bypasses.

Sexually, he is an unsure experimenter but on all levels he is a seeker of all that the world does not seem to have interest in.

Highly changeable, his drives fluctuate from day to day and with them so does his conception of who he is. He tries to internalize the future, envisioning all of the ideas of science fiction as probabilities, which he can personally experience. He likes people but he is a loner and cannot accept being personally bound by other people's ideas.

Karmically, he is living through many transcendental realms of reality outside of traditional norms.

RETROGRADE MARS
IN PISCES.

Here the individual spends most of his energies in the Third Phase in which he internalizes his past actions so that he can get a true reflection of himself. Often this causes great sorrow as he tends to blame himself for hurts he imagines he has caused in others. He prefers to withdraw from people rather than be responsible for the cause of their pain. His self-image is extremely low and he does not fight for what he believes is right. While he wants to be able to please others he often sees the futility of their plans and actions. Believing that humanity's difficulties are culminating, he does not understand that from moment to moment the world is only becoming, rather than being a final product. It is this lack of underststanding that causes him to be an escapist, rather than standing at the center of all that is around him. He tends to absorb more than he can handle because he perceives himself as being integrated with more than is necessary.

Karmically he is striving for a cosmic identity within himself and he must learn not to confuse the actions of other people's personalities with the essence of all he desires to be.

RETROGRADE MARS
IN THE FIRST HOUSE

Here the individual is most comfortable in Phase I of the Retrograde Process in which he tries to project himself into the future that he desires now. When he cannot make things happen instantaneously, he uses a great deal of thought projection bringing others into his Karmic desires until he ultimately believes he can actually make the future happen faster than he senses it would happen had he not taken a hand in it.

He is highly insecure, particularly about his sexuality, which in most instances seems to be fixated in his youth. Because of his impatience, he tends to go through much seemingly useless activity and behavior trying to create all that would naturally take place of its own accord. He is the isolated warrior of his past life desires remanifesting in his current incarnation, wanting others to join him and yet truly not allowing anyone into his own psychic space. Thus he lives much of his life alone.

He is overly self-conscious and sees much of the outer world as threatening to his own personal ego. This is why he tries to create situations of which he can prove himself the master. As a result he is often too aggressive with others, barely giving them a chance to think. In this way he is sure that his ideas will not be rejected.

He is continuing a past life Karma of building his self-identity and spends an emormous amount of energy defending any ground he has previously gained. In the present life he must learn to see and be in the "here and now" so that he does not over-react to situations which he himself has created.

RETROGRADE MARS
IN THE SECOND HOUSE

Here the individual spends much of his time and energy in Phase III of the Retrograde Process. He has many desires in life but he does not always have the drive to back up his desires by the hard work which will make them reality.

He can at times be very jealous of others when in fact he is only angry at his own failure to reach the potential he feels is within himself. He can brood and hold onto arguments that have long since passed. This occurs because he is so highly subjective that he does not always see the other person's point of view.

Karmically he brings with him into this life a strong desire nature which he will have to deal with on all levels. At times he tends to feel sorry for himself in order to gain the help of others. In this way he can replenish the energy he has wasted criticising himself for failure. He can pay lip service to others, acknowledging their achievements, but inwardly he does not truly give them credit. He really wishes that their achievements could have been his own. As such he tends to use a process of thought projection in order to identify with the deeds of others hoping through some unknown method to internalize, and make his own, the progress that they have made for themselves.

He tends to hold himself back sexually, secretly fearing that he may lose something. This is due to childhood fears stemming from early training that the world actually can take something away from him. He will reach happiness when he realizes that he is the creator of all he has to deal with in life, and that all he possesses or desires to possess is merely the collective symbology of all he values.

RETROGRADE MARS
IN THE THIRD HOUSE

Here the individual experiences a misalignment in his communicative processes. He tends to spend much time in

Phase I of the Retrograde Process trying hard to express himself in a way that will show him that he has actually made a dent in others. He offends people's sensitivities by being overly blunt, or using too much force while he impatiently tries to make his point.

In the horoscope of a woman this placement can often mean attraction to undersexed males or males that are unreachable. The female is not truly seeking the male energy on a sexual level for it can offend her own sensitivities. Instead she may prefer platonic relationships.

With this placement, Phase III of the Retrograde Process also comes into play as there is a very strong tendency to reflect on actions and thoughts long after the original experience has ended. Thus, on the personal side of life, all the individual goes through eventually becomes an endless echo.

He is living through a Karma of learning how to deal with his sensitivity to the outside world in the area of his personal relationships. He will reach happiness when he overcomes his need to personalize his environment. Eventually he can overcome the desire to an active part of everything that happens around him. When he masters this, he will experience the new sense of freedom that his souls has been asking for.

RETROGRADE MARS
IN THE FOURTH HOUSE

Here the individual spends much time in Phase III of the Retrograde Process in which he tries to relive the emotional experiences of his past. He tends to fight his own natural evolution as a strong unconscious desire to return to the womb keeps him rooted in some earlier stage of strong psychological conflict with one parent. As the individual goes through life, he seems to relate better with people whose ages are very different than his own. He can gain much strength from those older than himself while at the same time, tests his own strength on those younger.

This individual needs constant encouragement if he is to do something constructive with his life. He can be an enormous energy drain on others around him as he tends to need their energy to direct himself. All Mars Retrograde placements tend to drain energy from others, but here in the Fourth House, the watery lunar influence increases this effect to the point that the individual's inner needs can thoroughly exhaust those around him.

He is experiencing a strong dependency Karma and does not truly want to be on his own in this life. He tends to want to share his responsibilities with those whom he feels are stronger than himself.

Usually he will pick as friends people who are symbolic parent figures. It is through these people that he will blame one of his parents for all of the obstacles he cannot surmount in his life.

In the female, the avoidance of men is intensified by this house placement. She becomes a prisoner of her fears until she realizes that she has been negatively energizing past-life memories.

RETROGRADE MARS IN THE FIFTH HOUSE

With this placement, the individual experiences difficulty in expressing his creativity. On the sexual level his vibration alternately attracts and repels as he moves through the different Retrograde Phases. There is a tendency to be out of tune with the natural cosmic forces as the individual is trying too hard to be himself. Sometimes he feels that he is battling against the tide. But, he attempts to create those currents so that he will have something to swim against. In this placement, love affairs are hampered and the sexual drive does not flow smoothly. At the same time, any childlike qualities in the horoscope bcome magnified.

At one point in the life there will be energy expended in dealing with either a backwards male child or a younger person who refuses to fit into an expected behavior mold.

The concept of progress represents frustration as the individual constantly feels he should be doing something other than he is. He tends to mull over his setbacks in life rather than reaching ahead for new horizons.

He is experiencing the Karma of reviewing his entire creative process for much that he has created in the past has only brought him discontent. Now he must learn what is truly valuable to him in terms of his feeling of well-being. He will be able to do this best when he overcomes the unconscious feelings of superiority which have been feeding his ego instead of building his confidence.

RETROGRADE MARS
IN THE SIXTH HOUSE

Here the individual is caught between the conflict of how much he should do for others and how much he should do for himself. He tends to resent others telling him how to do things and yet he unconsciously wants their advice. Highly independent, he strives to be the ruler of his own life amidst a flood of external circumstances that dictate the direction of his energies. He is highly conscious of desiring not to be used by others, and yet it is exactly this thought that makes him keep inviting the very people into his life who can do that to him. He can be unusually cold where situations call for warmth as he has not yet fully learned how to trust other people's motives.

In areas of work he tends to underestimate the validity of his own output. He is seeking self-perfection though his deeds, and being overly critical of himself he also expects too much of others. In some instances this results in a tendency to judge others. It may be taken to an extreme where the individual's unconscious mind sees no other human being as having the ability to live up to full expectations. He can also cause himself to experience periods of sexual frigidity sometimes resulting in complete impotence. All of this is due to his living through the Karma of seeking perfection in action. And, as he tries to order the world around him, he slowly begins to order himself. Still, his approach to life is unduly harsh and on all levels, he would do well to follow the advice of Desiderata: "Most of all — Be gentle with yourself." When he learns this, his total view of others changes dramatically.

RETRGRADE MARS
IN THE SEVENTH HOUSE

Here the indiviual experiences a disorientation in his relationships with others. It is difficult for him to be married as the side of himself that he sees in a spouse is usually what he is least capable of accepting. In a female's horoscope this placement often indicates a past life hatred for men. In this life she will tend to look for reasons to justify her feelings. Often there is the expectation that a marriage partner is purposely trying to hurt her. There are very few individuals with this placement who do not carry an unconscious chip on their shoulder. Often this manifests in relationships that are highly argumentative, when the individual is willing to experience a relationship at all.

Basically, there is a mistrust of people. The individual is constantly on his guard against the possibility of being hurt. And, it is this very pre-programming that causes him to initiate the hostile feelings in others which proves his belief.

Karmically, this person has much to learn about the give and take of intimate relationships. His life is one continuous lesson for his ego so that one day he may align himself in balanced perspective with the effects he causes in others. Until he is able to realize this lesson, he will unconsciously experience in himself every negative reaction he has caused in others.

RETROGRADE MARS
IN THE EIGHTH HOUSE

Here the individual goes through a great deal of inner tension. He does not easily express the frustrations he feels as a result of the subtle way in which he is tuned to other people's desires. Often, he cannot separate the wants of others from his own, and this makes him hesitant at expressing the strong drive he experiences.

This placement often causes sexual difficulties as the individual inwardly feels the possibility of rejection which in his subconscious quickly associates with fears of abandonment, desertion, and death itself. He tends to alienate himself from many of the things that would bring him the fulfillment he thinks he is seeking. As such he feels separated from society. While he continues to deny himself fulfillment he is secretly jealous of other people. If used negatively this placement can be particularly destructive as the individual inwardly experiences the lower vibrations in the ether around him. On the positive side, however, the person can use this placement to bring forth the high ideals he intuitively senses at his deepest levels. This will transform both himself and those around him.

Karmically he is internally experiencing the desire nature of the world he lives in, and whether he chooses to act it out during Phase I or II, or watch how it acts on him during Phase III he is nevertheless confronted with overcoming his physical drives. He reaches happiness the day he is the master of his needs.

It is through the depth and perspective that the Eighth House affords him that he is given the ability to see the very core of his desire nature.

RETROGRADE MARS
IN THE NINTH HOUSE

With this placement, the individual experiences a great inner desire for freedom. Sometimes it is freedom from the bondage of other people's emotions, but on higher levels it becomes a quest to transcend human thought itself. In some, this manifests as a strong religious or spiritual quest bordering on fanaticism.

Marriage is unusual with Retrograde Mars in the Ninth House as the solitary qualities of Mars blend with the bachelorlike tendencies of the Ninth House, to make the individual desire to be a free spirit. In some instances the person is out of contact with his sex drive and can actually be projecting strong sexual impulses during Phase I of the Retrograde Process without having any conscious awareness of it. For the spiritual seeker, this placement causes difficulties resulting in the inability to control or stabilize the astral body. Here the guidance of a teacher is of extreme importance before attempting any form of astral projection.

Karmically, the Retrograde Mars in the Ninth House

gives a life that is somewhat of a lonely blessing. Through periods of isolation and circumstances which force the individual to deal with his inner attitudes and their effects, he is bringing lifetimes of his desire nature into the holy chamber of his higher mind, where once and for all he can achieve union with himself. As all of these desires are transformed and elevated to a higher plane he is able to finally complete the Shakespearean lesson: "To thine own self, be true!"

RETROGRADE MARS IN THE TENTH HOUSE

Here the individual finds conflict surrounding the decisions he must make in order to establish the security of his future. Many of his goals are based on the past and as such each step forward carries with it the full burden of his destiny.

He tends to feel that barriers are holding him back, but truly they are his own. Desiring to earn the esteem of his peers, he often checks and rechecks his actions to the degree that he seems to be a procrastinator. He will beat around the bush and undergo countless activities before taking the one step he knew he was going to take all along.

The career life tends to gravitate backwards in the sense that the individual strives early in life to reach the top of the mountain, then later on retraces his steps in order to realistically place himself at levels he should have dealt with earlier. Life is a succession of bypassed steps which are retraced later as he keeps trying to balance his foundations.

Karmically, this person is learning how to discover his future. And always, it is by retracing and filling the gaps in his past that makes his successful future more assured. As he grows older, he learns how to build in ways which are more meaningful to his ultimate purpose, rather than laboring under a past life illusion that he must conquer a world which is too formidable to master.

RETROGRADE MARS IN THE ELEVENTH HOUSE

With Mars here, there is a strong desire to daydream. The individual puts himself into states of conscious that allow him to relive moments in his past. He tends to shirk enforced responsibilities, but can handle them on his own providing no one is making him feel responsible. He can spend many hours either alone, or engaged in activities which to others do not seem practical. The truth is that most of his energies are directed towards his dreams, but he dissipates so much energy that he rarely is able to bring those dreams into reality.

Often he is detached from his sexual desire, and has a great deal of difficulty integrating it into the rest of his life.

The main difficulty is that he sees how quickly and easily his ambitions, hopes and dreams rise into the reality of his fantasies, but he knows how much effort it would take to bring these wispy desires into his everyday life. This is the point at which he blocks himself. The imaginary wall between fantasy and reality keeps most of his energies focused in his dreams.

Karmically, he is learning how to energize his ambitions so that after lifetimes of imagining he will be able to crack through the mental barrier which has been keeping them from becoming real. The difficulties he experiences in relating to others are merely the catalysts to get him to transcend his imagined inadequacies so that he develops enough desire to change his identification with the world. When he can do this, his actions will stem from a new and far more fulfilling perspective.

It is interesting to note that in this Mars placement, the erratic wispy qualities of the Eleventh House have less to do with the Retrograde Phases that the individual experiences than the actual zodiac sign that appears there.

RETROGRADE MARS
IN THE TWELFTH HOUSE

Here the entire desire nature is deeply rooted in past life Karma. Usually there has been unfortunate instances which have left the individual with a great deal of hidden anger. He tends to see it in others, because he is looking for it but he rarely recognizes it in himself. In the horoscope of a woman this makes relationships with males nearly impossible as each new male symbolizes in some way the one individual who in a past life hurt her deeply. As a result there is a great tendency to mistrust the motives of men since the individual feels there is little reason to expect better treatment in the future.

With this placement the life energy is being directed backwards in time with the hope of eventually finding where and what went wrong. Thus, male or female, it is very difficult for this person to live in the present.

All attempts to help the individual tend to fail until the person finds in the deep recesses of his consciousness what he thinks he is looking for.

The Karmic lesson in this life is learning to forgive. The person must understand that forgiving is impossible without forgetting. When this is learned the individual will no longer have to internalize everything and can set free those parts of himself locked in the past.

RETROGRADE JUPITER
ESOTERIC SYMBOL

Jupiter, the great beneficent giver is symbolized by the Crescent of Soul rising vertically from the Western arm of the Cross of Matter (♃). When matter and Soul combine harmoniously each is able to fulfill the other. It is interesting to note that the Western arm of the Cross is highly significant as the West always symbolizes maturity of that which has grown out of its birth in the East. In the normal symbol, the Cross of matter appears east of the Crescent of Soul. Thus, what the individual has materialzed early in life, forms his wisdom later on.

For the Retrograde Jupiter, the inverted symbol shows the Crescent of Soul in the East transporting the Cross of matter to the West. Thus, what the individual knows within his Soul early in this life (and as a result of past incarnations) is always what gives birth to what he experiences in matter later on. This can make the Retrograde experience a highly spiritual journey if the individual chooses to use it to its best potential. There is a type of incorruptible insistence on truth in the Retrograde Jupiter as it does not depend so much on the changes in matter that often sway the meanings of so many other planetary configurations. The individual is free to experience himself on a more pure level than if his truth depended upon his material existence.

At the same time, this configuration causes conflict with the outer world, as idealism takes precedence over practicality. A natural affinity for Jupiter's pure truth creates a distaste for the mundane everyday experiences of life.

RETROGRADE JUPITER
PERSONALITY

The individual with Retrograde Jupiter is a living truth

unto himself. His ideas about right and wrong, the morality of the world he travels in, and the fairness of other people's opinions has little effect on what he feels inside. In a powerful attempt to be righteous, this person develops his own unique set of standards. Usually, these are coming from past personal experiences early in this life as well as from other incarnations, and do not necessarily reflect mass consciousness, as much as they do the individual's privately formed conception of the universe.

He is highly conscious of different places and how much they are similar to each other. At the same time, he is conscious of different levels in his ways of thinking. Always a student of the mind, he seeks to experience an abundant richness within himself which he hopes will eventually equal the possibilities that are available to him in the outer world. Often this causes him much discontent, manifesting itself as an inner restlessness. He likes to get on with things, grasping the essence of an idea and relating to its importance rather than the details necessary to put that idea into practice.

If well aspected, he can be strongly self-motivated, but has to guard against trying to do too many things at the same time.

Basically, he is a free spirit. And, while he will conform to the ideals of society which are helpful to him, he struggles constantly to maintain his sense of individuality.

Some with this position have great wisdom, amounting almost to a prophetic ability. Quiet, unless spoken to, they can in a few words sum up the essence of long involved detailed projects, which would enmesh others in a multitude of trivia.

As much as the individual is capable of being conscious of, his intrinsic self-honesty is one of his most important identifiable characteristics. If poorly aspected, the Retrograde Jupiter can cause a person to hold grudges from past incarnations. In these cases, a long past desire to get even becomes reprojected onto new people in the present. Fortunately, this is the exception rather than the rule; for the Retrograde Jupiter affords the individual an opportunity to see himself through his higher mind. When he does this, some of his personal self-involvement gives way to a higher and more impersonal understanding. The development of richness in the inner being ultimately takes precedence over the desire to acquire riches in the outer world.

RETROGRADE JUPITER
KARMA

The Karma in the Retrogade Jupiter always deals with introspection through the higher mind. The individual must be able to justify himself to himself in order to feel that he is truly worthy of the respect and honor that Jupiter promises.

In some former incarnation there had to be a high regard for some religious or spiritual principle which the individual has seen violated. In the current life he feels even more determined to restate the value of this principle in his mind.

He has to guard aginst being judgmental of others as he sees an outer world vibrating to rules he cannot fathom. Still he must have patience with others, if he expects them to listen to the expression of his inner truths.

On another level, there is a tremendous amount of deja-vu experiences inherent in the Retrograde Jupiter. Times and places from the past all blend into a continuous present, such that at any given moment or in any given place, the individual is in touch with generalizing that time or place into all like times and places he has experienced. Thus, his consciousness expands through these two dimensions simultaneously, and often without limitation. He does not know how to bind his mind totally inward to a fine point focus. Instead, he absorbs the symbols of his thoughts from his environment, ultimately to learn that anywhere is home, and anytime is now! The more these outer symbols represent the truths he learned in a former life, the more comfortable he becomes.

RETROGRADE JUPITER
IN ARIES

Here the individual is most comfortable in Phase I of the Retrograde Process where the expansiveness of Jupiter fills the need for future expectancy. The difficulty is that the individual meets each new situation with preconceived ideas of what it will be like. As a result, he tends to try to control the circumstances in his life rather than flow with each new experience. With this placement there is a great thirst to re-experience the past: while the individual believes himself to be moving into the future.

There is often a strong sense of self-righteousness that permeates most of the thinking. This is accompanied by an abounding spirit of freedom on the most instinctual level.

The individual is striving for self-respect and has a tendency to judge others whom he deems of lesser moral worth than himself. He can become strongly opinionated when it comes to religious or spiritual identification and sometimes makes the mistake of categorizing individuals according to the philosophies to which they ascribe.

He has an inner restlessnes that keeps pushing him to sample all he has not yet experienced. He can also be childishly naive, not seeing the full situation or circumstance into which he is jumping. When he does see the full picture, he often has to pull himself back out. This type of behavior is extremely difficult in marriage for it offers the partner little stability.

Karmically, the individual is here to learn his own personal truths on the most basic of levels. He is continuing the lesson that being honest with himself is the key to his greatest security.

RETROGRADE JUPITER
IN TAURUS

This individual is most comfortable in Phase III of the Retrograde Process where he can reflect on all he has amassed in life. He concentrates much energy establishing that he is always right. This tends to make it difficult for him to adapt himself to other people's ways of thinking. He continually justifies his behavior and tends to be fixed in his philosophies as he stubbornly holds onto past concepts.

Very often he earns his living through some means which is now almost a forgotten art, such as being a tinker, a cobbler, a gourmet chef or a bookbinder.

Others see him as having an ego problem related to his unrealistic expectations from life. It is important for him to feel dominant and he deludes himself in many ways as long as he maintains a feeling of being in control of the circumstances in his external environment. Thus, he lives in a world which he has internalized. And, as a result, he falls under the illusion of thinking that all control over himself is really his control over others. At the same time as he thinks he is judging others he is truly judging himself.

There is much discontent centered around the material world as the individual keeps thinking he should be doing more with his life than he actually is. Thus, there is a tendency for him to weigh his accomplishments against those of the people around him and this only makes it more difficult for him to find himself. He lightens his Karma when he learns that the greatest truths come to him in the most natural ways and only at times when he is not trying to impress others or exert himself.

RETROGRADE JUPITER
IN GEMINI

This is one of the most difficult positions for Retrograde Jupiter as the individual is being taught to unite his higher and lower mind after lifetimes of conflict between the two. He is accustomed to basing his philosophies of life on the ideas of other people. Thus, he has learned to become unconsciously separated from his own truth while his philosophical values and ideas become strongly influenced by those who surround him.

He absorbs ideas from one individual after another without fully understanding what is true for him.

Experiencing restlessness during Phase III of the Retrograde Process where he is taking in other people's truths, he becomes anxious to redistribute every piece of information he has learned to those he is about to meet.

During Phase I he gives out much information along with misinformation, because he does not take the time to sort it out for himself.

In this life he must learn to focus his ideas and likes, and to observe how other people use them. Often he is an observer to other people's lives flowing through him. This causes frustration until he learns to settle into a practical outlook on life, distinguishing which truths expressed by others he should adopt and which he should disregard as not being applicable. Most of all he has to learn not to force other people to think as he does for his biggest problem is a tendency to believe that his attitudes work best for those he thinks he must teach.

RETROGRADE JUPITER IN CANCER

Here the individual is most comfortable in Phase III of the Retrograde Process in which he keeps trying to re-expand the child-like qualities from his past. He goes through life with a type of innocence believing himself to be unsophisticated. Thus, he has a great deal of difficulty during adult life because living in the present tends to pull him out of a time period which may have represented more freedom than his current reality. His concept of truth has always been more emotional than mental. And, as a result, he does not respond well to reason but instead tries to develop all his awarenesses from his emotions. This tends to re-emphasize his child-like qualities.

During adult life, there is a tendency to limit the expansive qualities of Jupiter within the confines of past experiences. As the planet's energies try to expand, the individual feels the Cancerian need to enclose. Meanwhile, the Retrograde motion of Jupiter pushes this entire conflict not only inward, but also backward into the past. Thus, the person goes through emotional and mental conflict at the same time. His memories are often exaggerated as he tries to correct all the past situations in which he did not fully express himself. And, he tends to repeat his experiences as if by repetition alone he becomes more secure in the correctness of how he handled himself in the past.

All of his past-life knowledge in his higher mind is now being tested as he is asked to live it out on his emotional level. Thus he must learn to faithfully believe and act upon his own truths.

RETROGRADE JUPITER
IN LEO

Here, Phase I represents the most comfortable experience as the individual can impress his zest for life on others. At the same time, there is a tendency to dwell in the self-pride of trying to live a moralistic life. He can be abrupt with others often interrupting their thought patterns desiring that he himself is heard. This is the type of individual who believes that he can teach everybody how to live. He likes to believe himself noble and may have actually lived through a former life in which he developed this characteristic by standing for some powerful idea or principle.

He likes to feel that everything he does in life symbolizes progress. As such, he keeps spreading himself out to increase the quantity of all he thinks is worthwile. He is attracted to all in life that gives the appearance of reward. Being highly independent he does not take advice well from others, but he does listen and at some future date will realize the truths that had been told to him.

One of his weak spots is the hastiness with which he jumps to conclusions during Phase I while only having to re-evaluate his judgments later. This occurs because the personal nature of Leo often blocks the impersonal awarenesses of the higher mind of Jupiter. This person can be more out of touch with his true nature than he knows. His philosophies and views of life tend to be different from those around him and it is important for him to learn that things can be different without being valued as better or worse. As the inflated ego which so often accompanies this position begins to diminish, the individual is able to experience one of the most beautiful cosmic views of the universe.

RETROGRADE JUPITER
IN VIRGO

With this placement, one of the most difficult problems the individual has to deal with is a lack of perspective. Many hypochondriacs have Retrograde Jupiter in Virgo. There is a conflict between the inner awarenesses of the higher mind, earned from prior lifetimes, and the present life experiences of mundane reality. He tends to box himself in from viewing the full picture. Thus, he sees parts of the whole and calls the parts he sees "all."

In relationships with others he is more an escapist from intimacy than a seeker of Jupiterian warmth. His idealism is so high that it is an impossibility for people to live up to his expectations of them. He goes through life with many specific ideals which form the abstract crystallization of what he is looking for. As a result, he tends to be strict with himself as well as others. Often considering himself to be above the baser aspects of life he is likely to develop an inflated spiritual ego. Through the purity of his ideals he inwardly comes to believe that he may be spiritually superior to others. This is where he traps himself, fighting his needs, and isolating himself from the realities of his existence.

In past incarnations he manipulated himself into the construction of unrealistic belief systems which he is now trying to live up to. He will reach contentment when he stops trying to be a symbol for all he thinks mankind expects of itself.

RETROGRADE JUPITER
IN LIBRA

Here the individual moves between all three Retrograde Phases according to the people he is with and the ideas he is confronted with. The concepts of fairness and justice have been so innately established in former incarnations that he does not always express all he feels, if he thinks it might hurt another person. If used negatively this placement can be carrying animosity from a former lifetime. In many instances the identity of the higher mind does not truly belong to the individual. Rather it is a collection of ideas from everyone he has known in his past. When he becomes truly aware, he will realize that he is acting out people's problems, exerting much effort seeking realizations which help him to solve a maze of conflicts which were never his to begin with. When he realizes this he is able to detach himself from all that had previously bothered him. Then he begins to learn that much of the restlessness he has been experiencing was not his own, but rather the desires of others for him to solve their problems. When he confronts his own personal ego he will learn why he not only accepted these desires but actually invited them.

Moreover, he likes to put himself in another person's place so that from such a vantage point he can develop a more balanced view of things. But the more he does this, the less he knows what he himself truly stands for. He is continuing a Karma of learning how to balance his higher mind instead of vascillating between viewpoints. He will reach his greatest joy when he is able to center his outlook on life.

RETROGRADE JUPITER
IN SCORPIO

Here much time is spent in Phase I of the Retrograde Process as the individual tries to project what he believes to be the truth to others. However, this is the one sign in which the person is also aware that what he has convinced himself of as the truth is not his complete truth at all. Thus, he can project what he superficially believes to be adequately complete while at the same time knowing that he is experiencing a deeper understanding on another level.

He brings into this life memories of struggling for honor and as he lives out his Karma he becomes a test for other people in this area. He can bring out the worst and the best in himself and others at the same time. This causes him to be a peculiar paradox for he is alternately understood and misunderstood, respected and degraded, loved and despised for all he represents to other people. His life is one of constant transformation as each day symbolizes new opportunities for struggle which help him to rise above the lower self which he now sees, but which still binds him in the current life. Very much the extremist, he stands for both heaven and hell at the same time. His ideals are usually very high, but during the first half of life he has difficulty pulling his higher mind out of the intense sexual drive which he brought with him into this life.

On any level, he is not one to be bound, for the depths to which he goes are usually reached alone and often completely misunderstood by others. He must have this freedom to explore the unknown reaches of the universe that keep calling him.

RETROGRADE JUPITER
IN SAGITTARIUS

Here the individual enjoys Phase I of the Retrograde Process. He is anxious to experience all that the world has to offer and finds it very difficult to settle down. His higher mind is attracted to a thousand different things at the same time and simultaneously tries to understand each one of them in a way which will not close him off from all the others. When he seems to be superficially light, he can be deeply prophetic, able to know the essence of something without having to spend a great deal of time talking about it.

When this position is used to its best potential, the individual is bringing with him a great deal of universal knowledge experienced in a previous incarnation. He usually has a high energy level and his mental restlessness makes him want to spread this knowledge wherever he goes. At the same time he has a habit of justifying his own righteousness and it is difficult for him to take the advice of others. He does not absorb ideas, but learns by experience. This position of Jupiter lowers the sexual drive and also tends to put relationships on a more superficial level.

In all ways this is the individual who likes to think for himself and, particularly during the second half of life, does not wish to be bound by conventional thought. His ideas concerning religion can be infinitely profound but rarely do they conform to the conventions and practices of any group, sect, or church. His Karma in this life is to live by his own knowing. He must learn to value that which he understands within himself rather than testing the values of others against his own ideals. If he develops himself, he can truly be a great teacher of all who are sincere seekers of truth.

RETROGRADE JUPITER
IN CAPRICORN

Here the individual experiences a constant conflict between Jupiter's needs for expansion, enthusiasm, and optimism, and Capricorn's tendencies towards restriction, sobriety and reserve. Thus, he must achieve a balance between these two extremes before reaching the vast wisdom that this placement is capable of. He is happiest later in life when he understands how to turn his higher mind to substantial values.

During his youth he often tries to act older than he is. Although he may be very wise, he is not heeded until later in life. In negative types, this placement can be very highly materialistic, especially when other chart indicators point to many personal insecurities; but when used on its highest level, it can be very spiritual. The individual may have a strong religious insight which he developed in former incarnations. In addition he has the ability to weigh things so that they ultimately are balanced from a centered perspective. In his life of action, however, he experiences a very strong stop and go vibration which does not always allow him to do all of the things he would like to do. He often paralyzes himself by considering things to the point that he is using more scope than he actually needs. In this sense he can over-exaggerate the importance of things by seeing too much of life as either supporting or negating principles he believes he stands for.

Phase III of the Retrograde Process is highlighted here as the individual is living through a Karma of maturing his understanding of himself and the world around him.

RETROGRADE JUPITER
IN AQUARIUS

Here the individual is most comfortable in Phase I in which he is anxious to experience the future. He wants to know all that traditional society has not yet explored. This is a very restless position for the Retrograde Jupiter as the individual is attracted to all the different paths which lie ahead of him at the same time. He is an idealist and a pathfinder. Although he is at times overly zealous, he can be a great contributor to the evolution of mankind.

This is a poor position for marriage as the person believes he needs his freedom in order for his higher mind to work at its best potential. What he really needs is mental more than physical freedom. And, the thrust towards this freedom does not come from current life situations but rather from his past life instinct to transcend mental and spiritual boundaries. He likes to live a life of enthusiasm and while he wants to help everybody he will push away anyone who dampens his spirit. It is hard for this person to direct his life in a singular direction. He is more comfortable darting here and there with a changeable purpose. His Karma is to apply his past wisdom to future experience. To do this, he will do much traveling and meeting new people from all walks of life through which he can share and express his knowledge. The Retrograde nature of the planet makes this more of a giving process than a receiving process; as he allows much less into himself than he wants to impart to others. Some with this placement experience claustrophobia, as they try at all costs to keep their life free of anything which symbolizes entrapment.

On the positive side, this is one of the best placements for the seeking of higher knowledge.

RETROGRADE JUPITER IN PISCES

Here the individual spends most of his time in Phase III trying to absorb his truth from the world around him. He can be deeply spiritual and mystical but he does not always say what he knows. He is inclined to spend a great deal of time sorting out the mystery of life which he senses. He finds people difficult to comprehend. In a past incarnation he may have spent time in the study of a religion or philosophy, for although he can't explain how he knows all he knows, he has a deep instinctual sense of life's true meaning. However, with all he feels, he still experiences conflict between his cosmic attunement and his ability to integrate with the rest of society.

He can be highly creative if he is allowed to do things his own way. One of his biggest problems is learning to stop doubting himself. Studies of Eastern Mysticism which substantiate the sense of non-involvement that he feels can help him to believe in himself more. He is living through a continuing Karma of learning to end self doubt. Through the use of his higher mind, he should avoid all possible entangling details which can keep him from the essence of his truth.

He doesn't like to judge people or conditions because he knows that nothing he thinks is really a conclusion but merely a way to another idea. The difficulty here is that he tends to lack discrimination and it is hard for him to keep his life and the people in it organized in his mind. His purpose being more universal than personal, he needs practical down to earth people in his life as stabilizing anchors.

RETROGRADE JUPITER
IN THE FIRST HOUSE

Here the individual spends most of his time in Phase I of the Retrograde Process anxious to experience the future through his own individuality. He is highly competitive, particularly with himself, for he is idealistic and not comfortable settling for less in life than he believes he can achieve. He wants to be recognized for his progress. There is a natural conflict in this position for the past life residue of Retrograde Jupiter propels the individual into many activities at the same time, while the true nature of Aries would rather be starting one thing at a time.

Still the combination of both the planet and the house gives the individual a high level of enthusiasm for making new beginnings. At times he has a tendency to over-extend himself and can leap before he looks. This makes him a natural pioneer, but one who is not always on steady ground. He moves through life quickly and does not like to waste energy.

In this life he is to continue expanding his self-awareness through the higher mind, but he must not appoint himself as one who sits in judgment of others. He knows a great deal about experiencing the outer self, and he can give this to others but he has to try not to scatter his knowledge too thinly.

This placement makes the individual highly independent and gives him a strong sense of his relationship to the

universe. Still he has to work at maintaining a reasonable
sense of proportion so that he does not make things larger
than they are.

Karmically, he is continuing a lesson in the evaluation
of self truth, for this is the one Retrograde Jupiter placement that forces him to personally live his philosophy.

RETROGRADE JUPITER
IN THE SECOND HOUSE

Here the individual keeps trying to re-establish a sense
of wealth, prestige, and justice that he has been accustomed
to in former incarnations. The higher mind is focused on the
value systems and in many cases becomes engrossed in the
physical side of life and enmeshed in materialistic desire.
Sometimes this is the individual who goes through a Karma
of judging others for having more than himself, but when
used constructively, this allows the individual to re-adjust
his values to the true meaning of life that his higher mind
knows. All he has to do is teach his lower mind to accept his
knowing. In most cases he feels that he is not getting
enough out of life. Sometimes he would like to make other
people's experiences his own, and he has difficulty knowing
the true differences between his own values and the values
of the outside world that he tries to internalize.

Preferring to think on a grand scale he has a tendency
to overestimate his needs. In some instances the individual
desires to possess things which should be allowed to be free
in the world. He even becomes possessive of the idea of his
own freedom.

Retrograde Jupiter placed here prefers to experience
Phase I but the phase the individual will spend most of his
time in is governed by the quality of the sign on the cusp of
the Second House. If the Second House is ruled by a negative
sign in earth or water elements, there is a strong likelihood
that the individual will be thrown into Phase III, which is
most inharmonious with the expanding qualities of Jupiter.

If the Second House is ruled by a positive sign, and in
the elements of fire or air, then the individual will spend
most of his time in Phase I. It is during this phase that the
individual tries to impress his values on the world while

during Phase III he takes the values of the world into himself. In both instances he is now living out the values of his past life attitudes.

RETROGRADE JUPITER
IN THE THIRD HOUSE

This is the most difficult position for Retrograde Jupiter, as the indivdual's past life ideas about the universe which he has been accustomed to are now affecting his everyday relationships. He is caught between the see-saw of trying to live the ideals he has developed in the past and sacrificing what he knows in order to mesh better with those around him. At times he can be overly blunt, for tact (insincerity) is foreign to his nature. He tends to be abrupt with people liking to cover a great deal of ground in a short period of time and yet he himself can be overly talkative. Spending most of his time in Phase I of the Retrograde Process, he is not always truly conscious of the people he is speaking to. He is more a giver of advice than a listener to others, and while many people filter through his life, he does not get attached to any one of them. He is so unusallly restless that he tends to scatter his own mental energies while silently judging others for doing the same thing.

He experiences a great deal of traveling and when he is not moving about physically he is moving mentally. The greatest difficulty with this placement is developing the ability to live in the human world filled with its apparent dualities and hypocrisy. Thus, he has to be careful not to develop an attitude of judging others.

In a highly evolved individual there is the capability of saying much in a few words, while in those people who are living through a more elemental Karma there seems to be an effect similar to a broken record in their speech patterns. Both are trying to get a message across to those people in their lives who are caught in lower mind.

In past incarnations, the Retrograde Jupiter was developed through use of the higher mind. But now the individual experiences frustration when he tries to express his understandings in the simple language his lower mind can comprehend.

RETROGRADE JUPITER IN THE FOURTH HOUSE

Here the expansiveness of Jupiter clashes with the protective qualities of the Fourth House as the individual tries to break out of the emotional walls he keeps erecting. Thus the infinite qualities of his higher mind become hampered by the insecurities in his emotional memories. There is usually a period during childhood where he is able to shine and as a result he keeps trying to recreate symbols of this period during his adult life. He is dependent upon others for appreciation. And, although he may not always show it, there is a strong tendency to be over-emotional.

He spends most of his time in Phase III of the Retrograde Process looking back to happier moments in his past. The negatively oriented individual tends to hold onto memories of past injustices. It is very difficult for him to be detached from his thoughts, because most of his awareness is of a purely personal nature.

The Retrograde Jupiter sometimes causes the individual to dissipate his emotional energy making it difficult for him to put his work or career in a single direction. He can become so intent about discovering the truth of all he does not yet understand about his past that he keeps looking at himself too closely to distinguish the forest from the trees. He needs the family structure as a foundation yet tends to find a great deal of scattered reasons why those close to him impede his progress. This person will do well to understand that most of the over-reactions he experiences are due to past life attitudes which are no longer applicable to his current environment.

Wherever he goes and whatever he does he is trying to win the praise of those close to him who can see the motives of his actions much clearer than he does. He will understand himself when he realizes why the need to hold himself down is stronger than his need to experience the outer world.

RETROGRADE JUPITER IN THE FIFTH HOUSE

Here the individual spends most of his time in Phase I

of the Retrograde Process. He is reaching outward to express
the creative attitudes he has developed in a past incarnation. He sees life on a grand scale and the boundaries of
conventional society as the stepping stones which he must
transcend at any cost. If the rest of the horoscope is strong,
this adds to a domineering nature.

In those charts containing many squares, along with
the emphasis in the fixed signs, Capricorn or an angular
Saturn, the individual tends to be oblivious to the advice of
others. He tends to invade other people's psychic space without realizing he is doing it. His own goals are very high but
he often over-estimates his ability to accomplish them. At
times he can expect too much from children because through
them he spreads the ideas that he is not capable of achieving
himself. He lives with a "don't stop me" attitude as he is
bursting forth to taste all that life has to offer. At the same
time his great sense of pride keeps him from embarrassing
himself in the eyes of others. He would rather dart from one
creative experience to another than be thought of as being
wrong by those whose esteem he wants. He lives by the
principle that if he can run through a rainstorm fast
enough, he won't get wet.

This is a difficult placement for marriage and relationships of a lasting nature as the individual's highest truth is
always related to his own opinion of himself rather than the
evaluation of criticism he might receive if he allows others
to know him too well.

Here the individual sense of identity is based on the gap
between the ideals set up in former incarnations and all he
creates in this life. Thus, he is truly the person who "is what
he thinks, having become what he thought," and in later
years he will know himself by what he has created.

RETROGRADE JUPITER
IN THE SIXTH HOUSE

Here the individual spends a great deal of energy per-
sonalizing the higher mind so that it may solve the problems
that he must deal with in life. He gets overly involved in the
starting of many projects which he may not finish, desiring
to have a finger in every pie. He is concerned with justness

in working conditions, and experiences difficulties with co-
workers and superiors by constantly trying to stand for
what he believes is right. Often he makes mountains out of
molehills and of all possible placements for the Retrograde
Jupiter this one is least able to experience the ability to look
at life from a cosmic viewpiont. While looking for the easy
way of doing things he tends to be distracted by so many
small points that it is hard for him to stay on a single track.
Here the higher mind is overly sensitized to the lower
thoughts of others. The individual can scatter himself by
paying attention to all the outer world details that his preconceived opinions bring to his attention. This is the person
who thinks he knows how the world works and yet, because
he thinks this, he always seems to miss the point. The problem is
that he tends to see his narrow awareness as representing the
total truth.

He can be overly moralistic in his expectations of others
but he sees people through the computerized qualities of his
higher mind as puzzles to be figured out rather than understanding them and their human frailties. He brings with
him into this life a Karma of expecting too much from a
world different than the ideals he has built in the past. He
reaches happiness when he finds a midpoint between these
past ideals and the practical realities that he deals with in
everyday life. At one time or another during this life he can
experience legal difficulties. This may be related to his emphasis on matters of lesser importance. He must learn to
establish priorities so that he can free the energies of his
higher mind from being taxed by needless, self-created
minutiae.

RETROGRADE JUPITER
IN THE SEVENTH HOUSE

This Retrograde Jupiter placement causes the individual to spend much time looking at himself as seen
through they eyes of others. As a result there is a tendency
to experience impatience to please others; although he is not
always sure of what prompts this. He can spread himself too
thin trying to gain the respect of those he admires and yet

with these efforts he knows that he is still unable to please the entire world.

In past incarnations he taught himself to stand for what he thought others would admire. Now he often feels that his sense of freedom is too dependent upon other people's ideals. He can never quite put his finger on all he knows about life. Answers seem to fly by as he tries to read other people's thoughts to understand his own truths. This person will argue more for the sake of upholding a principle which has the appearance of truth on a universal level than for his own need to win. Thus, he can become overly righteous.

Tending to put too much importance on the ideas that others present to him, he constantly runs into people whose philosophical attitudes towards life run contrary to his own. This individual is going through the Karmic lesson of learning that differences between right and wrong are strictly in the mind of the beholder. As he becomes more aware of this he begins to reach the consciousness of seeing how fruitless it is for him to make decisions or value judgments for other people. If married he is attracted to a partner who may well be overly righteous. Therefore on many different levels at the same time he is learning to balance the nature of truth through the many ways it is expressed from person to person in his life.

RETROGRADE JUPITER IN THE EIGHTH HOUSE

With this placement the individual has a highly developed sense of other people's values. Sometimes he has a tendency to try to give when he should be receiving. He experiences a great deal of sexual restlessness. It is the quantity of sexual experiences that he desires, but his needs, though he may think them physical, are decidedly mental.

He likes to reform other people, and knowledge from past incarnations leads him to believe that he has the wisdom which qualifies him to do this. He is interested in knowing what other people are like beyond and behind their facades.

However, he is reluctant to show his own true colors. There is a natural conflict in this position as Jupiter's desire for openness clashes with the Eighth House need for secrecy.

In business and commerce, this is an individual who must work for himself. There can be strong psychic tendencies along with a desire to use them in the most honorable ways. One of the great problems here is that the individual occasionally tends to judge others because they do not meet the expectations he has set for them. He does this a great deal during Phase III where his introspection tends to be expressed rather than withheld. Always questioning the validity of other people's knowledge, he stands very firm about what he himself knows.

Karmically, he is bringing with him into this life the fruits of a deep study of people, and the universe. But he must learn to understand that the deepest truths he seeks now will only come when he is not interpreting them on a personal level.

RETROGRADE JUPITER IN THE NINTH HOUSE

Here the Retrograde Jupiter is in its natural home. As a result, the individual is able to function comfortably in any of the three Retrograde Phases. At the same time, his life causes discomfort for those close to him. The Ninth House is the house of bachelorhood and with Retrograde Jupiter's natural instinct for freedom this becomes a poor placement for any kind of involved commitments of a lasting nature. There is a tendency to pull away from people as the individual desires to experience more and more of his natural environment in place of the sophistication necessary in living up to the social expectations of others. This individual goes through much difficulty putting what he knows into words. He is able to understand his higher mind, but does not always believe he is able to communicate his knowledge to others.

He has a great deal of difficulty in living through mundane situations and circumstances. In dealing with people, he usually knows instantly the point that he is going to make. However, he will avoid making it until he is sure the language he uses will be accepted by the other person.

He likes to move about and does not like spending too much time in any one place. As such he is very much the nomad, wandering through life to test the knowledge he has gained from former incarnation experiences against all present circumstances. Some with this placement have a very strongly developed understanding of God, while others who think their Souls are of a less religious nature express this through an explanation of how the mechanism of the universe works.

The greatest growth in this life occurs when the individual understands that the world around him is very much like the Tower of Babel. People are unable to communicate with each other because they have different conceptual understandings for the simplest words.

A person with this placement of Jupiter understands that the quality of communication with others is always less than he knows it could be. He senses the interruption in the steady flow of thought that is caused by language barriers.

His Karma is to know, to understand, to teach where he is asked, but never to impress himself on those who cannot comprehend his innate wisdom.

RETROGRADE JUPITER
IN THE TENTH HOUSE

Here the individual desires to present an honorable image to the world while at the same time maintaining his complete freedom of thought and action. He will often change his direction rather than exert himself because of his great need for expediency. He clearly sees the conflict between what he thinks the world expects of him and how he himself would truly like to be. This causes him to be a creature of extremes, vascillating between too much and too little self-assertiveness.

If well aspected, this placement of the Retrograde Jupiter can produce a great deal of wisdom which can be helpful not only to the individual but to everyone he meets.

It is interesting to note that during Phase I, the planet-

ary energy takes precedence over the expected house behavior pattern, such that the individual is able to overcome
the natural caution of the Tenth House. During Phase III,
however, he is not able to do this, and becomes highly introspective. But his most difficult experience is during Phase II
where the energies of the planet and the house are fighting
each other. During this time he lives through a high degree
of frustration amounting almost to a paralysis in action, for
as he keeps questioning the value of all he would like to do,
measuring it against the great scope of his wisdom, he keeps
feeling the impetus towards action for action's sake. Thus,
he is either not acting, but wishing he was, or acting and
wishing he wasn't.

He hates to backtrack over ground he has already co-
vered, and yet at times, particularly in relation to his
career, he must do this in order to pick up the pieces of what
he has left uncompleted. He is impatient to achieve and is
often more interested in the final results than in the steps
that get him there. He does not always live the same
philosophy he speaks, for in his living he may deeply believe
that the ends justify the means. However in his communication with others he does not like to commit himself to such a
philosophy. In addition he becomes uncomfortable if someone tries to pin him to any specific philosophy. He can become defensive of his ideas and attitudes for he has strug-
gled long and hard to build them. He likes being in control
and actually must be, in order to live out the Karma of
standing for what he believes regardless of opposition.

In some instances, the entire life stands for one attitude
or idea that comes from some shining achievment in a
former incarnation.

RETROGRADE JUPITER
IN THE ELEVENTH HOUSE

Here the higher mind is stimulated by the Aquarian
need for exploration. During Phase I of the Retrograde Process the individual is highly curious about all he has not yet
tasted. He brings from the past a need to freely experience
many diverse situations to expand his understanding of life.

He may be continuing to seek a goal he has been chasing for lifetimes. Often, there is a tendency to be lax about the details of life. He may also spend a good amount of time living dreams. Still he is idealistic and tends to have an open-minded attitude towards life.

Often his goals seem unreachable as he tries to think beyond human possibilities. This makes him highly individualistic. He becomes discontented at the idea of settling for less than what he knows is possible. And he tends to rebel against all that would bind him to traditional thinking.

He can attain unusual honor among social groups providing he is allowed to do things his own way. He brings with him into this life the Karma of understanding the true nature of his dreams. In this way he can build a purposeful reality by knowing the reasons for his goals, hopes, and ambitions.

Of all the positions in the Zodiac he is the most freedom-oriented. He lacks practicability and is unhappy about accepting the responsibilities associated with intimate relationships,. But, in spite of all of this, his thirst for understanding is so great, that he eventually becomes one of the very few individuals who touches the truth of the cosmic law.

RETROGRADE JUPITER IN THE TWELFTH HOUSE

Here the individual spends much time soul searching in order to reach his inner being. He often makes the mistake of thinking that others can help him know himself better than he already does. In truth it is easy for him to know his inner self, but often it can be so easy that he attempts to use the other planets in the chart thinking that he must seek some great mystery beyond what he thinks he is capable of comprehending. The wealth he achieves through life is built upon an inner sureness of himself which, although it does not always appear to mesh with the outer world, gives him unbounded understanding of his inner being. This is a very Karmic position for Jupiter as the individual will learn ultimately to understand the truth about his past incarnations, and thus the reason for his present life. He is sometimes too harsh on himself and he must learn to judge himself fairly through his higher mind if he is to be comfortable with his soul. This placement makes life very introspective, as much time is spent in Phase III of the Retrograde Process.

Still, an inner wisdom, coming from unseen spiritual guidance pervades the entire life style, as soon as the person is ready to draw on his inner wealth. Most of the time his knowledge is beyond the words he can find to communicate all he knows. But, he does communicate very well on telepathic levels.

RETROGRADE SATURN

RETROGRADE SATURN
ESOTERIC SYMBOL

The Saturn symbol is composed of the Cross and the Crescent ($\hbar$). Here matter and the form side of life must be united with the Soul's sincere desire to express itself. Thus, all that the individual does he crystallizes into what he is adding to his Soul nature. The value of things is seen by the Soul itself which must discriminate between what it wants to partake of and what it wants to avoid. As the individual looks at life through his Saturn he may appear somber and serious but what he is doing is considering the relationship between idea and form. He concerns himself with his ability to see how much of his Soul he can actually manifest with matter. Thus, it becomes important for him to view his deeds as a reflection of his true inner being.

The Retrograde nature of the planet causes him to experience much of this reflection as an inner struggle between the consciousness of his ideals, their practicality, and his ability to live up to them. Thus, for many, the Retrograde Saturn becomes their conscience and guide, blending as a mediator between the perfected higher being and how much it must still learn in order to live here on earth.

RETROGRADE SATURN
PERSONALITY

The individual with Retrograde Saturn is intently serious about completing whatever he has left undone in his past. He tends to want to go backwards in order to fill any gaps in what he had hastily considered finished before. As such, he tends to be thoughtful and steady. At times he may seem overly cautious or too frugal, but any reserve on his part is based entirely on his need to conserve substance for purposeful use. He does not believe in waste or extravagance for he has experienced that in other lives. Now he is deeply appreciative of everything he learns or receives. Often he feels an inner debt to God which manifest itself as a powerful sense of gratitude for all he sees around him.

He tries to teach others, who are less knowledgeable or experienced than himself. Yet, he is unsuccessful if they have not gone through his past life "fall from heaven" and his great struggle which has now earned him his way back. As a result of this, there is a built-in maturity in the Retrograde Saturn that one could not have achieved without great personal struggle and sacrifice.

RETROGRADE SATURN
KARMA

Retrograde Saturn always indicates a continuing Karma from past incarnations. Whatever the lesson, the individual is unusually slow in bringing it to completion. Thus, in this life he needs to carry the extra weight in his soul of a former life so that when the two ultimately combine there will be enough evidence for him to fully understand his true mission. Much of what he does in this life is a repeat of what his Saturn already stands for. But now he faces circumstances and situations that are slightly different. The Retrograde action of the planet can make him feel its restrictive force, particularly if he tries to escape the weight of its lesson. But, if he flows with it, understanding that through the patient guidance he is receiving, he is slowly being led to identification with something higher than he may have imagined, he can truly appreciate the workings of God's beautiful universe through this planet.

Saturn is one's teacher and when it appears Retrograde, the indivdual has experienced similar teachings before this life. As the years unfold there is an enormous amount of wisdom that steadily pours from the Retrograde Saturn.

Of all the planets, it is the most natural and comfortable in its Retrograde position, for it affords the individual a kind of second chance to improve on the relationship formed between his soul, the circumstances he was faced with in a past incarnation, and how these were understood. Now under the gentle guidance of Saturn, he is able to put into form all that he has learned in the past.

RETROGRADE SATURN IN ARIES

Here the individual is bringing into his present consciousness all he has learned about himself in past lives as he experienced the ways of dealing with responsibility. As such he tends to be firmly independent and does not like others to see any weakness in him. Whatever is important to him in life he achieves on his own for he has learned how to pull his ideas together and direct his energies towards a purpose. This configuration adds power and strength to the horoscope as the inner fortitude of the Retrograde Saturn steadies the Arian ambition and gives it meaning. The individual eventually becomes a kind of father to himself insofar as he is his own best guide through life. As he matures, self confidence becomes strong and the usual Arian displays of ego are less pronounced. The individual bases his sense of self-worth on all he has built within him in the past. At some time in a former life he was forced to stand on his own two feet at a very young age. As a result, he comes into this life with a strong sense of how important it is to experience self-development.

This placement also tends to add patience and consideration to what might otherwise be an impulsive nature. He will spend his entire life trying to become his own Master.

Phase I of the Retrograde Process is highlighted here as the individual tries to project himself into a future which will assure his self-esteem. Karmically, he is using the formed strength of past-life attitudes to help him make a new beginning in this life through the house ruled by Aries in the chart. And it will be crystallized ideas, philosophies, and judgments that have structured themselves in his Retrograde Saturn that will eventually become his tower of strength.

RETROGRADE SATURN IN TAURUS

He can be unusually attached to things, places, and ideas that seem to remind him of all he was accustomed to in the past. With this placement the fixed nature of Taurus is strengthened as habit patterns of lifetimes repeat themselves again and again. Sometimes there is difficulty in expressing what the individual knows, as language is not his best asset.

Here Phase III of the Retrograde Process is strongly highlighted as the individual tries to recreate all that he values in matter. He is interested in being able to structure his life so that he ultimately achieves a sense of feeling that he has earned his security. Until he knows this he may experience the fear that his safety and security could be taken away from him. Thus, he has to work to make his inner sense of well-being a permanent part of him.

The interesting thing about Retrograde Saturn in Taurus is that it gives the individual the ability to actually reverse any negative physical Karma he has accumulated in the past. In its place he can build anew all that is meaningful to him. In order to do this he channels much thought into re-evaluating all of his past burdens until he realizes how much his Soul has been accustomed to doing things the hard way. Until he transcends his out-dated approach to life he can be a very negative thinker. As such he may harbor anger at how difficult life seems to be for him while it appears to be so much easier for others.

RETROGRADE SATURN IN GEMINI

Here the individual experiences difficulty in communicating. He often knows what he wants to say, but not how to say it. He is continuing a past-life lesson in relating to other people. In trying to find means of gaining the acceptance and approval of those he wanted to please he collected one crystallized thought form after another. Now, in this life, his tiniest thoughts carry with them the full weight of all the past thoughts he has attached them to. Thus, it is difficult for him to reach the very essence of understanding that he seeks without having to sift through all the Saturnian thoughts that he has connected together.

People with this placement tend to quietly worry about others. Saturn Retrograde in Gemini believes it is a guardian of the thoughts of others. At the same time, there is a great deal of repetition in the individual's own thought processes. He constantly seeks to be sure of himself, but the more thoughts he collects, the more he doubts what he knows. Interestingly enough, this doubt is very good for him, because it makes it easier for him to release the thought forms he has crystallized in the past.

Thus, his Karmic mission is actually an unlearning process through which he can again reach the simplistic state of understanding what he once knew, before he began burdening himself with the "excess baggage of educated opinions."*

It is during Phase I of the Retrograde Process that he actually complicates his life by collecting too much thought. Then, after going through much worry and confusion in Phase II he is finally able to release all that is of no value during the final phase.

RETROGRADE SATURN IN CANCER

Here the individual spends most of his time in Phase III of the Retrograde Process in which he keeps dwelling on emotions which burdened his past. He tends to be slow making progress in life as he feels he constantly has to be sure of himself. The need for security is high. Unfortunately, the more energy he spends trying to free himself of his emotional blocks, the more he actually recreates the very blocks that wall him in still further. To be free he must allow himself to flow through the blocks without using force. There is space in all apparently solid matter which water is able to permeate.

In many instances, a strong past-life attachment to a figure who represented protection and safety is transferred to a parent or older authority figure in this life as the individual does not consciously understand how he can live without a protective womb. When he does try to come out of himself he is not sure that he will be fully accepted by others. Thus, he tends to wall his emotions in as if to save them for the one individual he may meet in the future who will be symbolic of the past security he has given up.

*Zolar: The Encyclopedia of Ancient and Forbidden Knowledge.

He tries to keep the concept of familiarity in his mind. Even when he travels he keeps identifying each new place with a past that he is already comfortable in. In this way he can move through life with the feeling that he is securely rooted, no matter where he is or who he is with.

Because he experiences living in a world that seems to be changing around him, it would be better if instead of trying to make his present fit into his past, he realizes and accepts within, the past securities he has known so that he does not have to continually seek them in the outer world. In this way he can fulfill his Karma of everpresent birth.

RETROGRADE SATURN IN LEO

Here the individual is confronted with a Karma of achievement. He cannot feel worthy inwardly unless he can outwardly produce all he feels he is capable of. It is important for him to feel important to himself as well as others. He strives to achieve command of all he does. And, the obstacles he feels he must surmount are nothing short of grandiose. Often he will suffer for the sake of others, for he gets much fulifllment from assuming other people's responsibilities. At the same time, he can be domineering and willful.

He is bringing into this life the Karmic residue of power; the ages in mankind's history where might made right. And he is overly concerned with being right in the eyes of others. He wants to be respected and will go out of his way to defend positions or crusades for causes which make him appear to be more in command of himself.

He makes a strict parent and a rather formidable adversary as he is always more concerned with the power of the position he is standing for than actually defending himself. In order for him to live up to expectations that were had of him in the past, he tries to assume charges of those around him.

Thus, he is living a life of assumed responsibility rather than one of natural existence. He must learn how to meet responsibilities within himself, first, and not assume them for others.

RETROGRADE SATURN
IN VIRGO

This placement indicates a person who is trying to reach his past ideals. He continually delves within himself to assess how much of his life is living up to what he believes it should be. Although he may seem to be overly concerned with the details that shape the structure of his life, it is ultimately through these details that he is able to create the neatly ordered universe that can make sense to him. He sees the world through all of its separate parts. Then he tries to fit these parts into all that has formed within him from the past. Thus, he internalizes what he believes to be correct segments from the outer world. Then from these segments he builds his structured life.

He thinks that in order to know himself he has to understand the workings of everything that touches his life. The main problem is that due to the Retrograde nature of Saturn he inadvertently pre-programs his perception of things so that they can fit into his ready-made concepts. This makes him unusually rigid and tends to decrease his Virgo mutability. In his work he can be unusually efficient, particularly when he knows others are depending upon him for order and efficiency.

Karmically, this is the individual who is forced to live the idealized world he would like to see around him. Once he becomes sensitive to how unrealistic some of his expectations are, he can become more comfortable with the world as it is. The perfection which already exists will then become apparent to him. Because of the enormous amount of observation of other people's lives inherent in this position, the individual goes through Phase III of the Retrograde Process before he can actively express himself in Phases I and II.

RETROGRADE SATURN
IN LIBRA

In this placement Retrograde Saturn adds inner maturity to the otherwise indecisive qualities of Libra. The individual feels a strong responsiblity to others. Often he experiences their Karma more than they do themselves. Naturally this can throw him off balance. In the long run his judgment is quite sound and he is able to steady himself.

A born peacemaker, he is often thrown into the middle of opposing people or ideas. From this position he tries to bring harmony by establishing a balanced third point which expresses the positive aspect of both sides.

He has the ability to actually change and alter the Karmic directions of those people he comes in contact with. As a result of meeting him they begin to re-evaluate and weigh proportionately their own past beliefs and the direction they had been moving in. Thus, for many, this placement gives an opportunity to take an objective look at their purposes in life so that their validity may be re-assessed. For the individual with Retrograde Saturn in Libra life is a series of turns and twists until he understands that his Karmic mission in this incarnation is not for himself, but rather to help direct others to a more balanced purpose. This is done by setting an example of balance through harmonizing the apparent opposites of thought. He brings this about by finding the essential unity of human ideals.

His adaptability allows him to change from one Retrograde Phase to another depending completely upon the need of the moment. Thus, he is truly one of God's most versatile and valuable helpers.

RETROGRADE SATURN IN SCORPIO

Here the individual experiences the meaning of life on its most basic level. He has very deep insight, most of which comes from his own personal experiences. Constantly living on the brink of destroying himself, he keeps throwing away all he attains because of the lack of deep meaning he ultimately sees in almost everything. He believes that behind that which he can perceive at the moment is the reality he knows exists.

The building of his substance takes place deep in his subconscious and the momentary fascinations of life do not fulfill him in the least. He is always conscious of an inner cosmic reality which keeps drawing him to its center.

In the outer world he is very fixed in his attitudes and there are few who can sway him from whatever purpose he feels he has. He can be a crusader trying to transform the society he lives in, a rebel against orthodox tradition trying to transform himself, or a seeker of truth wishing to transform humanity. It all depends on the level of Karma with which he comes into this life.

Usually, this Saturn placement is outwardly a Phase I experience while inwardly a Phase III experience acts as the undercurrent which motivates all apparent action. Thus, the indiviudual's inner reflections about his place in the society he lives in becomes the stimulus for the ways in which he would like to transform it.

RETROGRADE SATURN
IN SAGITTARIUS

Here, the life is built on past principles. Highly independent, the individual cannot be lead by the advice of others.

At times he seems overly opinionated, but the strength with which he expresses his ideas to others does not truly reflect his own adherence to them. Whatever cause, principle, or mission he appears to stand for, it is constantly changing. He tends to represent man's need to withdraw from whatever traditions appear to have outlived their usefulness.

Generally the true nature of the individual does not come out until mid-life, after he has tried the conventional ways of living and found them to be too restrictive. He would rather be his own disciplinarian than follow the dictates of others who he feels don't really know what is best for him.

In many instances he seems to grow younger as he ages. He eventually learns how to make light of things which were once burdensome to him. He has to watch a tendency to judge others, for he can alienate himself by doing this. By and large, however, he does try to be fair in his inner appraisal of people.

He is living through a Karma of learning how to allow his higher mind to understand and correct his past mistakes. In later life he finds himself doing all that he knew he should do when he was younger. Here the backward effect of the Retrograde is stressed as the individual is living Phase III of the Retrograde Process through most of his adult life, after finding that Phase II which he tried to live in his younger years did not seem to fulfill him as much as it did his superiors.

RETROGRADE SATURN IN CAPRICORN

With this placement, much time is spent in Phase III of the Retrograde Process as the individual tries to restore a past image of himself. He is accustomed to hard work and thrives on the possibility of one day looking back at jobs and projects that he has done well. Having a unique ability to lock out interference, he can better than any other zodiacal placement, direct his life towards a useful purpose. This is the gift which makes him capable of achieving so much. At the same time, he works backwards, i.e. not starting anything before he can conceptualize the finished product. This increases his practical approach to life. He can be highly reserved and often secretive as his inner planning tries to shut out external distractions, which might otherwise sway him from his self-appointed direction. He is especially good at picking up pieces from the past that society has overlooked and making a great life's work out of such seemingly useless fragments. This is because he cannot tolerate waste.

Karmically, he is living through a mission of accomplishment, but what he achieves in the outer world is far less important than the amount of inner meaning these achievements bring to him. He will complete in this life, whatever he has collected data for in a past incarnation. With the maturity of this position, his Soul is now ready to bring to fruition lifetimes of labor along a given path. Whatever house this appears in, is an area of life which he can (if he wants to) bring to Karmic completion.

RETROGRADE SATURN IN AQUARIUS

Here the individual is highly unique and independent.

He is interested in all the different things that life has to offer. His rules and traditions are outside of conventional norms as they represent the accumulation of all he has collected out of many radically different sources.

His originality of ideas, however, is solidly formed and although he likes to listen to all new pieces of information which will increase his storehouse of knowledge, he still does not change the basic underlying attitudes which he has formed in a past incarnation. Thus, while he tries to reach for the future, he still maintains a strong link with the past. If anything, he can actually drain those who are mapping out the future, because of his constant need to fit new discoveries into past concepts.

Because of the erratic qualities of Aquarius, he experiences all of the Retrograde Phases. Unbelievably curious he seeks to attain so much understanding of everything that he actually uses up the freshness of all that is new. Thus, he makes the unconventional old before its time. When he does this, he is quite unknowingly forcing society to accept the new by adding notes of tradition, conventionality, and yes, even boredom to it. The more he adds weight to everything new by playing it down, the more society wants to possessively protect it. Thus, his Karmic mission is to follow the forerunners of the future and be a bridge between all they discover and all mankind needs to know and use now.

RETROGRADE SATURN
IN PISCES

Here the individual spends most of his time in Phase III of the Retrograde Process as he keeps going over the essence of his past. He imagines his life burden as heavier than others, and tends to dwell in past sorrows long after he could have confronted and surpassed them. Lacking in confidence, he tends to give up on life too easily. The endurance he needs in order to bring out his creativity always comes from the inspiration of others. But, the real approval he needs is less from those around him than from his own realization of his inner sense of worth. Never being one to overtake the world, he is rather timid in his youth. As he grows, however, a power from within begins to emerge from the very essence of his Soul.

Part of his life is based on the reality of his current existence, but most of his inner being is already formed before this life. He has accomplished and surpassed many of the tests others have yet to endure. As a result, the lack of confidence experienced during youth becomes replaced by a powerful inner knowing as he grows in closer contact with his Soul.

Karmically he is drawing on the inner strength he has in order to deal with the outer world. Usually this position indicates great spiritual fortitude and the person does not have to be aggressive in life to prove his own self worth. Much of the understanding inherent in this position is non-verbal. The individual does not speak of the many ways in which he knows he is capable of helping others. He has a gift of inner guidance which he earned in a former life and this is the source of much of his creative potential now.

RETROGRADE SATURN
IN THE FIRST HOUSE

Here Phase I of the Retrograde Process is highlighted as the individual tries to find an impressive and formidable identity structure that the world around him can vibrate to. He tries to impress his reality outward because he desires feedback when he will later experience the other two phases. Something in the personality structure is greatly lacking, and as such there is a strong tendency to compensate. Usually there is a series of barriers between the individual and the people he would like to get close to.

A type of non-trusting attitude pervades the entire identity structure due to some past life situation in which he felt shut out or closed off from what he tried to reach. Now, instead of facing that, he tries to be important so that others will recognize him and perhaps relate to him in a way in which he will not be hurt.

This individual is highly sensitive even though he doesn't appear that way on the outside. Karmically he is learning how to stand on his own two feet and because this process is so slow he is highly fearful that anybody might try to knock him down before he has built his own foundation. Most of all, he spends his entire life building a castle of rules, which will ultimately be the structure of the identity he wants to achieve.

RETROGRADE SATURN
IN THE SECOND HOUSE

Here the individual is learning Karmic lessons about possession. In former lives he tried to crystallize all that was of value to him and now he tries to reapply those values to his current situations. Spending most of his time in Phase III of the Retrograde Process, he keeps collecting all that offered him past security. Thus, he is highly resistant to change. He tends to be watching the world from some place in the past where he once felt comfortable. As such, he stubbornly keeps precipating all that holds him back. The truth is, he doesn't really understand how his values fit into the world he now sees around him. Thus he experiences a barrier between what he feels and what he is able to live, and this can actually alienate him from all he wants.

Unless Venus is unusually well-placed, this position tends to block the expression of love. Every time the individual tries to give his love to another he is brought to question whether or not he is fulfilling his values. He always senses something is wrong, but he has difficulty putting his finger on it. Usually this is due to an underlying sense of guilt in terms of how he has treated people in relation to things.

He will reach happiness the moment he clearly realizes how untrue he has been to himself in the past.

RETROGRADE SATURN
IN THE THIRD HOUSE

Here there is great difficulty in communication. The individual cannot easily put his thoughts into the words he knows others will understand. Part of the problem is that too many of his ideas are formulated in black and white and he doesn't realize the many shades of grey that exist between the two.

Because he tries overly hard to get his thoughts across to people, while inwardly believing that they are not as

receptive as he would like them to be, he experiences great
difficulties in all of his relationships.

Often he blocks his conscious mind from being sensitive
to the signals which come from deeper parts of him. As a
result, he is not fully integrated within himself. The parts of
him that he is able to consciously understand are in great
measure a facade of thoughts, rationalizations, and the con-
structed ideas that he finds socially acceptable. No other
Saturn placement crystallizes all current life thought forms
as strongly as this one.

There is so much importance attached to each thought,
that the individual actually weights himself down with one
question after another. The interesting thing is that he has
already pre-programmed the answers. This hampers the
learning process, for what is sought after is only what will
substantiate what has already been formed solidly in the
belief system.

Spending a great deal of time in Phase II of the Retrograde Process he goes through conflict between the input and
output of information. He has spent so much time in former
lives learning how to learn, that he actually has become a
victim of habits that lead him to fill himself with more information than he really needs.

Karmically, he must learn how to develop a clear priority of thoughts, throwing away all that is unimportant,
while learning to express better that which is meaningful.

RETROGRADE SATURN
IN THE FOURTH HOUSE

Here much of life is spent in Phase III of the Retrograde
Process as the individual keeps trying to find what is
bothering him at the very roots of his Soul. In spite of all
else he does, this keeps much of him inner-directed nearly
all the time.

There is an unresolved Oedipal conflict in the personality. It is composed of many problems stemming from early
childhood. A strong persistence of emotional fixations can
lead this individual to follow one track of crystallized feelings for most of his life. Because of this, he tends to carry a
lot of astral matter, and can be burdening to others by the

sheer weight of his inner emotional conflicts. Even when he gets answers to his questions, he seems not to know how to use them in the resolution of his problems. He tends to block himself from seeing the deep meanings of things, which in truth would set him free.

For many with this placement, there is the continuance of phobias developed during the early years which must be overcome if the lingering attitudes which block self-awareness are to be transcended.

Of all the Saturn placements this one is the strongest in terms of keeping the individual tied to his past. He can literally spend forty years trying to resolve burdens that he felt were put on him at too young an age. In his own adult family, he keeps re-enacting the traumas of his youth, but often he does this on an unconscious level so that others around him are hardly aware of the roles they are being cast into.

The Karma here is to learn how to tolerate the emotions of others in close contact without internalizing or carrying guilt, blame or responsibility for all that has occurred in the past. As soon as the individual can learn to live in the present moment only, he will notice how many of his worries are unreal.

RETROGRADE SATURN IN THE FIFTH HOUSE

With this placement the individual feels a strong need to overcome obstacles that he perceives in his creative process. He keeps feeling that he should be doing more in life than he actually is, but he tends to delay much of his productive output until later in life. He feels a need to create something of lasting value in order to feel a sense of purpose. In some cases he will have to bear a heavy burden in terms of paying a Karmic debt to a child. Still, if he can do this, it will help him to establish the sense of purpose he is seeking.

He tends to stymie himself, actually slowing down any real progress in life, because he has inner fears of commitments. Still, no matter how much he would rather be an observer of life, he keeps falling into one situation after another where the full weight of responsibility is put on him. The more he seeks pleasure, the more responsibliity he finds himself carrying. In great measure, this is to teach him what life is really about.

Love matters prosper slowly for there is a great deal of maturing to take place before an intimate relationship can flow smoothly. The individual has many self-doubts when it comes to expressing his creative abilities. He doesn't really think he can measure up to other's standards. Thus, he forbids himself much that he really needs. He can turn probabilities that he could attain into such obstacles that they become too remote from his life for him actually to reach them.

He worries too much over childhood inadequacy fears which are still operating in his unconscious.

Karmically, he must learn how to stop perpetuating fears which block his creative flow. As soon as he can do this, he will not only overcome many of his obstacles, but he can also make an important contribution to mankind.

RETROGRADE SATURN IN THE SIXTH HOUSE

Here the individual feels a strong responsibility to others. He would like to be able to carry their burdens for them, if only he could.

At work he can be a fantastic organizer, shaping together all the disordered pieces that others do not know how to handle. At the same time he must learn not to run himself down, for he sometimes tackles more than he is comfortably able to handle. Being more of a doer than a thinker, he can literally run himself ragged trying to meet the expectations others have of him.

He likes to live with a sense of purpose, but he does question the origin of everything. This is part of his struggle to find out if man's life is pre-destined or if it is of his own making.

He must learn that although he is involved in a mission of service to others, it is not for him to decide what the specific needs of those around him are. He can get so bogged

down in trivia, by trying to fulfill everybody, that he loses
sight of the fact that only God is the real fulfiller.

He brings with him into this life a sense of dedication,
and for those who need direction his presence alone will help
them to find their goals. He must be careful during Phase I
of the Retrograde Process not to try to impose his goals on
others. Working better as the servant, he can function
smoothly during Phase III where he can review other
people's dilemmas to try to help them crystallize solutions.

RETROGRADE SATURN
IN THE SEVENTH HOUSE

Here, the Karma of marriage is learned at its fullest.
The individual often feels that his spouse is holding him
back. Even if unmarried, he will feel the weight of others
trying to get him to retrace his steps in order to gain a more
balanced and mature view of himself.

In some cases this placement indicates marriage to an
older partner who the individual may actually have known
in a former incarnation.

The biggest lessons center around the establishment of
harmony with others. He knows this, but his ego tends to
rebel when the going gets heavy. Nevertheless he has
learned through former incarnations that his real security
comes more from others than it does from himself. He needs
to feel protected. As such, even though he may often complain that marriage is boring, he knows that it is a stabilizing
anchor which keeps him from what might otherwise be a
lifestyle that is too hectic for him to experience and learn
from.

Karmically, this Retrograde Saturn placement gives
the individual the opportunity not only to work out childhood problems with the dominant parent by selecting a
similar-type mate for marriage, but also to share one's life
unfoldment with another, who in many cases appears to be
the backwards student, but who in reality turns out to be
the teacher. Thus, there is much to be learned from this
position if the individual allows himself to experience Phase
III of the Retrograde Process, through which he can be re-

ceptive to ideas that seem beyond his present maturity level.

RETROGRADE SATURN IN THE EIGHTH HOUSE

With this placement, there is much Karmic inter-changes with others. The individual tends to live other people's values in order to transform himself through what others have found to be worthwhile. As a result of past in-carnations, he has not yet learned a sense of purpose for himself. Thus, he wavers under the influence of his marriage partner and the other people in his life.

Sexually, there is restriction bordering on impotence owing to many Karmic fears which have been collected. There is much worry about this and repeated tests of sexuality almost to see if it's there. Many females with this placement had unpleasant sexual expereiences with an adult male during their early childhood years. This is the primary cause of frigidiity, guilt, and shame later on. In all cases, the sexual nature is rooted in the past.

The attachment to whatever is of mature value in others, gives the individual a great deal of confidence and common sense in the world of business, where his Saturnian cautiousness works to his practical advantage.

For the mystical student, this Retrograde Saturn position enables the individual to recall old Karma in order to develop new insight into old ways of thinking. Thus, he is able to be reborn as he can release forever old value systems which were never really his, but which he had tried to conform to in the past.

Since many of the values of the world are highly dependent upon the sexual evolution of the race at any given moment, this Eighth house Saturn position reflects a great deal of world thought through the individual's own personal life. Much time is spent in Phase III of the Retrograde Process as old traditions are retested against society's current standards.

Karmically, the individual is reviewing and transforming all that mankind has crystalized as past tradition.

RETROGRADE SATURN
IN THE NINTH HOUSE

Here Saturn finds a special home as it brings the individual into contact with the already-formed parts of his higher nature.

In many instances, he brings into this life a mature sense of wisdom that was developed in past incarnations. Regardless of his I.Q level, which he often feels is not what it could be, he has more wisdom than knowledge. Still, the Retrograde nature of the planet often makes him doubt himself and causes him to look harder for his understandings than he really has to; but this is only until he learns that all of the effort he puts in to try to think out solutions to problems is merely a part of his learning how to stop thinking. The moment he does this, he begins to notice that the answer is always there!

For many this Saturn position represents a long spiritual journey at the end of which the individual will find self-respect before his God. He will begin this journey by trying to read every book, attend every lecture, and literally try to grasp every higher thought in the hope that by the sheer possession of much knowledge, he will find what he is looking for. In the end, most of what he learns comes to him through much more natural means.

Should he try astral projection, he will be aware that his astral body is fairly heavy and has a tendency to disturb others unless his projections are extremely gentle.

Karmically, he is a seeker of the first order and is continuing a mission in this life which he began before. He experiences all of the Retrograde Phases as he keeps forming substance to his philosophical and spiritual beliefs, thereby transforming his collection of opinions into a very real sense of knowing!

RETROGRADE SATURN
IN THE TENTH HOUSE

Here Saturn is in its natural home. The individual spends much time in Phase III of the Retrograde Process reviewing the prestige and dignity he has attained in the past. Through this he determines his present opinion of himself. As such, he is status-conscious, particularly in his peer group. Unusually, he is judging himself in terms of past peer groups and how he measures up to or surpasses them now.

This is a position of dedication for the Retrograde Saturn. The individual feels a strong sense of responsibility and has to account to himself for everything he does. Thus, he is deeply concerned with seeing his life as some sensible formative structure which has followed more or less a reasonable track from the beginnings of his memory to the present moment. He tends to be rather crystallized in this respect, and reason and logic may elude him if it means deviating from his pre-programmed sense of duty to his self-image. This effect comes from those rare moments when he very privately experiences Phase I of the Retrograde Process.

The only way he can be swayed is if it means the possibility of improving his self-image in the future, as long as nothing of his past is destroyed in the process. Karmically he is trying to establish a sense of principle which he did not have thoroughly formed in past lives, and does not truly have in this life in areas other than his career, public image, and sense of duty to society.

RETROGRADE SATURN
IN THE ELEVENTH HOUSE

This is the position of the idealist. The individual has to deal with the crystallization of his dreams, hopes and goals. It is not enough for him to simply dream them as others do. He has to feel a sense of their coming to fruition before he can feel like an important person to himself. As such, he has the difficult task of learning how to blend his reality with what he would like to be his reality. Often this involves taking on the responsibilities of friends, as the individual's own life is not truly wide enough to include the reality of all of his dreams. For this reason he must widen it by bringing to himself those individuals whose lives symbolize those parts of his dreams that he is not willing or able to live out himself.

The Retrograde Phases change with this Saturn position

depending very much upon the other people in the individual's life. He is a very good advisor because all he suggests to
others is really that which he himself would do if he were
living the other person's life. In a sense, this position creates
a kind of "Spectator Karma", in which the individual is less
at the center of his own life than at the center of his dream,
which may well be a lot of other people's lives. Thus, no
matter who is really in his life, it is that which they stand for
which is ultimately more important than who they really are.
Even if he tries to draw important people to himself, this
individual is more unconsciously concerned with the what
and why of their fame than the actuality of who they are.

RETROGRADE SATURN
IN THE TWELFTH HOUSE

Phase III of the Retrograde Process is highlighted here
as the individual becomes deeply introspective. His greatest
concern is that he develops an inner truth which remains
unchanged under the pressures of the world or his personal
fortunes. Thus, he is building a foundation within himself,
and as such will have to draw on knowledge he has accumulated in past incarnations in order to make his foundation
solid. He may feel a great debt toward those less fortunate
than himself. And there is no question but that he himself
has felt the heavy weight of Saturn personally in past lives.
He now sees his responsibilities more as a cosmic debt to the
universe rather than a personal debt to one specific person.

Many with this Saturn position become so overly introspective that they begin to question the value and importance
of everything they do, and their identification with the collective importance or lack of it, in the world around them at any
given time greatly affects their outlook on life. More than
anything else, the lesson here is to be true to oneself, from
whatever vantage point vision   is possible.

Of all Saturn placements this is the one which brings to
the individual the greatest amount of inner maturity. Whatever the outer world asks of him, his strongest feeling is the
security he feels inwardly by being true to his God.

RETROGRADE URANUS
ESOTERIC SYMBOL

The symbol for Uranus (♅)is formed by two opposing Crescents of Soul connected through the Cross of Matter. As the wayward wanderer of the heavens, Uranus has always been connected with all that symbolizes man's unique abilities to reach beyond the mundane. In order to do so, he must break convention at all costs, often tearing himself in half in the process.The Soul Crescents pointing in opposite directions remind us of the lunar symbols of the waxing and waning Moon; each presenting a different side of life, like the two sides of a coin which although they are so opposite in nature cannot exist without each other.

The Cross of Matter stands at the center of this tug of war, symbolizing all that man has already established as his traditional foundations. From the arms of this Cross, the two Soul Crescents constantly pull in opposite, and as yet uncharted directions. The nature of the Soul, seeking to explore the unknown, forces the individual to make continuous decisions between the stability he already knows and the positive and negative possibilities of all he has not yet tasted.

Thus, the symbol for Uranus stands less for man's unpredictability than it does for his striving to free himself from the matter or form side of life, which hampers all of the existential possibilities he innately knows he can reach.

When the planet is Retrograde, one takes this as a personal crusade, feeling deeply within oneself a responsibility for the progress of mankind as a whole. The symbol when inverted puts the two Soul Crescents closer to earth. Thus, it is not enough for this individual to liberate himself. He must feel the freedom of everyone in his life space before he can be contented with the fact that the liberation of his own Soul has penetrated into the matter of all he sees around him.

RETROGRADE URANUS
PERSONALITY

The individual with Retrograde Uranus displays a rather unique personality.

On his innermost levels he is a rebel against all that binds him. If he is a fearful person, he may exhibit claustrophobia. If he is a daring person, he will attempt to topple all that he sees as having outlived its usefulness. He cannot be contented to just go along with life, for there is too much he sees that can add richness to mankind if only society would shake itself loose from all of its false security anchors.

He will actually worry if others begin to accept him too much, for then he feels he has lost a great part of himself. In this respect, he will from time to time lose many friends and acquaintances, sometimes jobs, and romances all because the strangeness of his ideas is often too difficult for others to accept. And yet, years later, when society is advocating all he once stood for, he no longer has an interest in whatever advanced theories or attitudes he was promoting at the time. Thus, he is very much a forerunner of the future. Because of this, he can experience a great deal of loneliness, but he would never give up his gift of originality for the companionship of others. He knows that above all else, his Soul must be free. Anything which impedes this freedom he will shake from his path.

For those who are able to understand him, he is one of the most fascinating people to listen to; for he is literally filled with all of the ideas that mankind needs for the future of the human race.

RETROGRADE URANUS
KARMA

On a personal level, Retrograde Uranus plays havoc in human relationships. The individual experiences an inner changeability that often makes him hypocritical to himself. His mental and emotional levels often fight each other so that he may know certain things which should lead him in the direction which his knowledge points to, but at the same time, he feels other things which may lead him in an entirely different direction.

He is living a Karma of learning how to express the inner freedom that he brings into this life. And, he must not be bound by trying to make sense at all times to others, or even himself. A free spirit does not always appear to make sense, nor should it. The fact is, that a logical continuance of common sense in an individual is more of a Saturnian trait, bound by the rigidity of order, discipline, and the pointing of oneself towards specific goals. But, the individual with Retrograde Uranus is not living such a Karma.

In order to explore his inner being, as well as so many other realms of understanding that mankind as a whole has not yet reached, his path is often long and crooked. He darts this way and that seeking the formulas that make the world work. Still, he knows that his quest is a never-ending process, for each new discovery leads to still another question. He can be extremely happy so long as others do not try to force him into molds of thinking and behavior patterns that he has already transcended due to the meaningless roles they play in his perception of the grand scheme.

He has learned how to be independent in former incarnations, and now he must use this independence to rediscover and understand the reason he originally wanted it.

RETROGRADE URANUS
IN ARIES

Here the individual spends much time repeating changes within himself that were begun in another incarnation. He is highly individualistic, independent and unique. He lives for spontaneity within himself, trying to be free of the barriers that would keep him bound in any kind of tradition. He is a very intense rebel against anything he sees which is overly traditional, or too solidly formed to allow room for him to improve on it. He is a great seeker of excitement and is usually ready to give up any security he has for the promise of some kind of intense stimulation he has not yet experienced. This makes it difficult for him to be contented for any great length of time with marriage, partnership, or even jobs or a career which can get to be too boring.

Sometimes he can become a leader of unpopular causes.

Whatever he does, he must prove to himself that no one person or idea (other than of his own choosing) can bind him. He is probably one of the most interesting and original people in the Zodiac. Spending most of his time in Phase I of the Retrograde Process, he is a true pioneer, seeking to explore all that society is overlooking. He spins fast with little patience for anything or anyone that could impede his forward motion. This enables him to be free of the limitations of society's educated opinions.

His Karma is to walk where there are no footsteps in front of him, forming new mental beginnings in everything he does. He must constantly draw on past life awarenesses so that he can apply every ounce of ingenuity he has developed in order to make these new beginnings. Though at times he may walk a very crooked mile, without him there would be very little progress for mankind.

RETROGRADE URANUS
IN TAURUS

Here Phase III of the Retrograde Process is highlighted as the individual keeps re-evaluating all he has already lived through. Financial and emotional security becomes shaky, but this only makes the individual more determined to establish himself. At the same time he experiences a strong sexual interest in anyone that seems exciting or different.

In past incarnations he developed crystallized conflicts in his value systems which now must be broken if he is to make progress within himself.And while these crystallized parts of him keep luring him to hang onto the safety and security of his past, the Retrograde Uranus keeps lifting him from his lower self, but putting him through circumstances that make him aware that much of his sense of safety and well-being is built on false foundations. Thus, he constantly shifts between calm serenity and the exciting exploration of new boundaries which may have little or no promise of practical outcome.

In many ways, this Uranus position causes an individual to want to have his cake and eat it too. He likes to be married but at the same time believe he is free. He likes to work in a steady job while convincing himself that he is not bound by it. He likes to follow one religion while thinking within himself that he truly has no obligations to it. Thus he is untraditional, in a very traditional sense. When confronted with the opportunities to be truly free from marriage, job, religion and all other parts of the form nature of his life style, he quickly jumps back into the womb of safety that Taurus always seeks.

Karmically, this placement occurs in the charts of individuals whose Souls are trying to break up crystallized thought patterns from former incarnations, but who are not yet ready to detach from the primary importance they have put on the physical side of life.

RETROGRADE URANUS IN GEMINI

Here the individual experiences a highly active mental life. He keeps changing from one Retrograde Phase to another as he tries to find the identity that makes him the most comfortable. Being unusually nervous and erratic, he is highly influenced by the external thought in the world. This makes it difficult for him to stick to any one topic or any one project for a great length of time. He has so much of an interest in exploring all of the mental possibilities that occur to him, that his life becomes a literal smorgasbord of scattered ideas, and attitudes. Not having enough confidence in the uniqueness of his own thoughts, he tends to identify with the originality of others.

There is much instability with this placement of the Retrograde Uranus. Sometimes the individual can actually cause himself harm by trying to understand so much of what is outside the periphery of expected normality that he can actually lose his reality perspective. This occurs as a result of his internalizing belief systems which not only distract him from the progress he thinks he would like to make, but which also throw him far from any realistic goal-oriented approach to life. The crux of the problem is that he is unconsciously highly gullible.

Realizing this, he should exercise care in areas of hypnosis or other deep mind techniques which tend to take him too quickly into levels of his being which he is not yet ready to handle.

He is so highly mentally activated that even his interest in sexuality takes on more of the coloring of mind exploration than it does any physical or emotional fulfillment.

As one of the most curious people in the Zodiac, he is living out the Karma of the investigator who through life after life could not decide upon any given chosen path as being the right one for himself. Now he keeps shifting his direction, momentum and speed so that he tries very many different things but never really settles in any one of them. In this respect, he knows people from many different walks of life, each one representing something he would like to try.

If he works on raising his consciousness, he will one day realize the mental gymnastics he has been using for eons which have been keeping him from experiencing himself.

RETROGRADE URANUS
IN CANCER

Here the individual experiences changes in his family structure. There is constant emotional upheaval stemming from experiences that he is unprepared for. In the female, this placement sometimes indicates a child born out of wedlock. When the question of abortion arises, she is confronted with her Cancerian need for motherhood conflicting with the Retrograde Uranian need for personal freedom.

Whether male or female, the disharmonious emotional makeup is caused by constantly questioning and analyzing everything to the point that the individual never truly allows a settled emotional life to fully develop.

Spending much time in Phases I and III of the Retrograde Process he desires instant answers to all his feeling, but in his search he tends to move right past his answers. He can become highly intense trying over and over again to solve problems that he has actually lived through many years ago. His biggest difficulty is synchronizing himself in the time dimension where he keeps re-evaluating his past in the hopes that it would create a better future. And yet, because he does this, his future actually becomes the mirror image of his past. There is always emotional frustration as he tries to rebel against his family while still benefitting from all that it gives him.

The Karmic lesson here is to learn emotional contentment. From experiences in past incarnations, the individual has not yet developed within himself a true sense of gratitude for all that has been given to him.

RETROGRADE URANUS
IN LEO

Here the individual experiences an unusually high energy level. Most comfortable in Phase I of the Retrograde Process, he is truly the original commander of his life. He rarely allows himself to be led by others and hardly ever asks for outside advice. When used negatively, this can become a very bigoted, self-centered position for the individual doesn't like his ideas to be questioned by others. Thus, he can live his entire life totally off the track, missing the point, hearing every one of his friends, neighbors, and relatives telling him the same thing, yet never listening.

Experiencing constant turmoil between the unique and the conventional, he will identify from moment to moment with whatever gives him the strongest feeling of individual power. He can become overly aggressive, losing control of himself whenever his ideas are threatened.

He is a very difficult person to live with, as he constantly tests the loyalty, sincerity, and honor of those around him. At the same time, he refuses to conform to norms established by those he sees unconsciously as being of lesser value than himself. People tiptoe around him in fear of triggering him off while he continues his mental game of shattering everyone's ego but his own.

Karmically, this individual is power hungry. As such he is constantly discontented with whatever he has. Even if he searches for spiritual answers, he grows overly zealous, too possessive, and much too prideful of whatever awarenesses he reaches. The Retrograde nature of the planet turns his discontent inward at the same time as he telepathically on an unconscious level pours out the residue of his unhappiness onto everyone around him. His biggest area of disharmony is that the rebellious freedom loving nature of the Uranus Retrograde must be lived out within the traditional confines of Leonian principles. And, no one can solve this dilemma for him, for if he is to truly reach the power he knows he can have, he must find its source within himself!

RETROGRADE URANUS IN VIRGO

Here the individual experiences Phase I of the Retrograde Process as he tries to mentally order everything within himself by planning the future order of everything he sees around him. His ability to think clearly is fantastic, but he tends to jump to conclusions. Knowing how things should be, he has to learn the patience to apply himself to life in an orderly fashion before he can create the kind of world he perceives.

He tends to go through life on large reservoirs of nervous energy. There is a kind of immediacy to all he does. Above all, he is a doer. The problem is that he doesn't always stick to things long enough to either fully complete them, or reach the deep level of satisfaction that he could achieve from them.

In the positive sense, this position can add a touch of genius and clairvoyancy to the horoscope. The awareness level is high and instantaneous. Insight is strong when it comes to practicality for others. The individual, however, has more difficulty in seeing himself.

Karmically, he brings into this life a multitude of ideas, which he must learn how to put into practice. He must overcome his tendency to constantly flit from one thing to another, using up all the joys of life so quickly that he actually becomes jaded at a young age.

If he turns his consciousness to spiritual levels, he will discover that he is one of the most aware people in the entire Zodiac.

RETROGRADE URANUS IN LIBRA

Here the individual experiences all three phases of the Retrograde Process. His life is very much controlled by all the imbalances he perceives in the people around him. He desires peace, but actually it would bore him. Still, when he experiences too much excitement he wishes for peace. To find the balance between these two he moves from one person to another, often acting out their Karma because he is so unsure of his own. Decisions are difficult, and he would rather have them made for him than to actually take the responsibility of putting his own life in the direction of his will. Thus, he can blow like a leaf in the wind according to the values and ideas of the people he associates with. He tries to maintain his own sense of independence amidst all of this, which results in a kind of impartial fairness towards everyone he knows. It actually bothers him when situations or circumstances force him to take sides in any issue.

He is highly skilled at looking at himself through the eyes of others. Unfortunately this is not the same as looking at himself through his own eyes. Thus, the ultimate balance he achieves is based more on what he perceives outside of himself than on what he can reach inside of himself.

Always caught betwixt and between people of differing ideas, attitudes, and behavior patterns, he tries to maintain his equilibrium while not toppling the values of those he loves.

He is the Karmic chameleon of the Zodiac. Liking to be of constant service to everyone who needs him, he must not really be too attached to any specific values of his own, except that he is here to give love and whatever awarenesses he has learned, to whoever needs him.

RETROGRADE URANUS
IN SCORPIO

Here, the Retrograde Uranus finds a beautiful home, as it keeps bringing light into the greatest depths of the individual's quest for understanding. He is never content to leave anything at face value, but rather keeps digging to find the roots of all that seems unsolved. He is a genius when it comes to research. In addition, he is highly psychic, knowing the essence of things in an instant. He has little patience, but he discovers things so quickly that he really doesn't have to apply himself for very long periods of time.

On a personal level, he goes through many sexual changes in life. During one period he may be seeking all kinds of excitement that he has not yet experienced, while during another he may turn to complete celibacy. In whatever he does, he is an extremist, never settling for a middle-of-the-path to life. His energy level is high and quite intense, for when he knows the truth he is not about to let others sway him from whatever independent course of action he has chosen to embark on.

This can be a highly spiritual placement, particularly during Phase III of the Retrograde Process during which the individual can reach his awarenesses of the universe within himself. He doesn't kid himself, or live in illusions, but rather takes great pride in seeing things the way they really are.

He brings into this life a great ability to understand much of what the rest of society doesn't even know exists. Karmically, he is living this life in order to play a very active role in shaping the world he lives in. He is not to sit back and complain about all he sees wrong around him; but rather to be one of the leaders in transforming human consciousness.

RETROGRADE URANUS IN SAGITTARIUS

Here the individual spends most of his time in Phase I of the Retrograde Process. Itching for future and distant horizons not yet within his reach, he keeps aspiring for all that is symbolic of whatever is beyond the mundane things in life. As such, he has difficulty stabilizing himself in his practical day-to-day living. He cannot focus on small things or details for very long, because he gets bored easily. He needs constant new stimulation to satisfy the very active thirst for life that keeps driving him on.

He loves to travel, and if he's not doing it physically then his mind is mentally roaming through all the unknown regions he has not yet explored. Still, he is not necssarily a deep person. Instead, it is scope, breadth, and bigness that he is seeking.

This is a rather difficult position for marriage, since the individual feels threatened when he is restricted. He needs room to explore all the possibilities he finds in his higher mind, and any attachment to one person would deny him the advantages of superficially experiencing many.

This same attitude carries over into most of the areas in his life. Following one religion would violate the Uranian need to be fair to the others coupled with the Sagittarian drive to experience them all. He goes through career changes for the same reason.

While all this may seem to indicate that he is a very scattered person in terms of other people's values, he sees it as fulfilling his insatiable curiosity to experience all there is to life. And, when he is allowed to follow his numerous directions (which don't always seem to relate to each other) he is able to maintain a very high level of enthusiasm.

This enables him to be a kind of Karmic messenger, bringing to everyone he meets, the piece of life they need at the moment. Thus, while he is enjoying himself in each new discovery he is actually a spreader of seeds that others will care for, nurture, and help to mature into what will become man's future consciousness.

RETROGRADE URANUS
IN THE FIRST HOUSE

This is the most highly individualistic position for the Retrograde Uranus. The individual has little interest in the rules or traditions of the society he lives in. He identifies with all that is new and unique and will go out of his way to rebel against anything which cages him or makes him appear to be like others. He is striving to establish his own sense of uniqueness so that he can distinguish his own personal identity from the myriad of identities he sees around him. This is usually expressed in Phase I of the Retrograde Process in which the individual experiences a great fear of waiting for others to pull him into their realities. He tries to express himself as quickly and spontaneously as he can all the time.

This is a very poor position for marriage inasmuch as the individual's nature is highly unpredictable as he tries to break ties with conventional society. There is continuous change until the person understands that his true purpose is not to dedicate his life to any principle or course of action which might smother his spirit of adventure. Unquestionably he spent another life learning how to explore the vast regions of existential possibilities which allow man to follow his insatiable curiosity. Now he continues to do this, but in a world that is wider and with more possiblities than he had experienced before. As a seeker of the first order, he will sacrifice much of the comforts of traditional society in order to be free to discover that which exists just beyond the limits of his contemporaries.

RETROGRADE URANUS
IN THE SECOND HOUSE

Here the individual experiences constant changes and fluctuations in his values. The principles he stands for do not stem from any other particular origin. Because of this, it becomes difficult to know what he truly stands for.

Usually, Phase I of the Retrograde Process is highlighted here, but the nature of the sign can change this influence. In a positive sign, the individual is trying to express all the differences which exist within himself, so that others may experience the same things. In a negative sign this whole picture takes more of an after-the-fact introspective coloring. Thus, one individual is impressing his reality in the universe while the other is reacting to a universe of differences.

In either case, the financial outlook and the individual's attachments are hectic situations which never seem to offer the stability he would like.

Karmically, there is a fear of commitment to be mastered. Rather than pinning himself down to any one specific track in life, this person likes to taste bits and pieces of different possibilities which he might one day ascribe to — after he has sampled everything! He is an explorer of ideals, values and the reasons or purposes most people live for. Unfortunately he is not willing to adhere to anything he discovers. Thus, he can be of great assistance to others, while not personally realizing the true values within himself. When he learns to be impersonal, he will see the light of life's true meaning. Thus, the commitment he will eventually make will be based on what the universe impersonally shows him as its truth.

RETROGRADE URANUS
IN THE THIRD HOUSE

This is a highly ingenious, yet very rebellious position for the Retrograde Uranus. The individual absolutely insists on being different than the society in which he lives. As such his ideas and principles keep changing along with his erratic behavior patterns. The totality of all he is comes to represent so much of what his traditional environment is not. He even changes the Retrograde Phases so often that here too it is difficult to see any real pattern to his life style. Due to this, however, he is one of the most original thinkers in the Zodiac. His inventiveness is without cause or definite purpose and he is unhampered by the boundaries which tie others down.

At the same time, this placement causes difficulty in getting along with others in work or personal relationships because there is so much insistence on expressing individuality no matter what the cost.

Being a rapid learner, there is a tendency to skip over things. Thus, the approach to understanding is helter skelter rather than thorough. In later years, this person will undoubtedly go back over much that he raced through earlier.

Karmically this placement adds a touch of genius and/or madness to the rest of the horoscope. The individual spends his entire life learning how to learn, and although his sources may be bits and pieces from many different individuals, phrases from many books (the complete texts of which he does not have the patience to read), and spots of different experiences, his life has a tremendous richness to it in terms of the scope of knowledge he touches.

RETROGRADE URANUS
IN THE FOURTH HOUSE

In this position the individual experiences strong emotional turmoil. He wants to break from his symbolic "birthright," be it the religion he was raised in, the moral or ethical values he was taught, or the individual personalities of his parents. The more he focuses his inner thoughts on these things, the more he keeps vibrating to whatever the original conflict was. He seeks individuality, but only within the framework

of some type of family structure or organizational boundaries to prove to those that bind him that he is truly free.
Thus, he lives the illusion of freedom within his self-created
prison walls.

Much time is spent in the introspective Phase III of the
Retrograde Process through which he reviews all that he has
already lived through. On the emotional level his concept of
time is quite different from chronological reality. Even when
he occasionally experiences Phase I he jumps out of his shell
only to look behind to make sure that his womb is still
following. Karmically he is experiencing a great deal of self-
doubt coupled with moments of extreme self-confidence. As
he goes through life he vascillates between one and the other
trying to find the place in which he hopes he will be emotionally comfortable. Until he is exactly sure of where this is, he
clings tightly to the shackles which he says he is throwing off.

RETROGRADE URANUS
IN THE FIFTH HOUSE

Here the individual is dedicated to the creation of an
original life style which enables him to blend with the world
he lives in and at the same time feel himself as a uniquely
independent part of it. He has a fear of being trapped by
society and as such tends to jump the gun by throwing himself into Phase I of the Retrograde Process in which he can
avoid all that would make him appear conventional by establishing his unconventional identity first. He is an ingenious
thinker and as such has no difficulty following the ideas of
others. His attachments are unique and he prefers living
with another individual rather than being married.

One of his greatest talents is his ability to excite others
about ideas that were on the edge of their consciousness but
which they felt were too unorthodox to explore.

Karmically he is one of the most independent Souls in
the entire Zodiac, for not only is he concerned with his own
personal uniqueness, but also with the originality of all he
creates. Unquestionably, in some previous life he must have
experienced what it felt like to be forced into some mold that
was very different than what he felt inside him. Now he goes
out of his way to be sure that he stays his own person at all
costs.

RETROGRADE URANUS
IN THE SIXTH HOUSE

Here the individual can express great innovations in his daily work routine. He can take the most mundane chores and discover uniquely interesting ways of dealing with them. At the same time, he is highly sensitive. This makes him particularly open to influences in the external environment, which in turn make him feel the need to be active at all times as he can become internally restless.

No matter how much this individual may say that he wants peace, he tends to vibrate to all that takes life from the mundane to the exciting. Thus, if peace is really his intention, he has a powerful tendency to defeat himself. One of his greatest concerns is wondering why other people do things the way they do. This train of thought leads him into constantly trying to understand the motivations of everyone around him.

Karmically, he is a great innovator on the physical plane. Past incarnations have given him a great understanding of the relationships and processes of the physical world. Regardless of which Retrograde Phase he is in at any given moment, he is constantly seeking to understand, or looking to apply his understanding, so that he may be of better service to the world around him. All he has to learn is how to stay calm and collected in the process.

RETROGRADE URANUS
IN THE SEVENTH HOUSE

This individual is experiencing the need to develop self-reliance. As such he has a tendency to attract those people upon which he believes he may lean. But, because they are "Uranian" in nature, their ultimate unreliability forces him to grow stronger within himself.

This placement for the Retrograde Uranus denotes a reaping of Karma, particularly in the areas of marriage and relationships, until the individual learns how to grow more impersonal in the definition of his needs. He must come to understand that in past lives he grew to expect too much from others and that the continuation of such a pattern is unrealistic as well as unnecessary.

Often, this position indicates more than one marriage. It also indicates difficulties in maintaining a level of sexual warmth with the opposite sex. Relationships grow into a kaleidoscope of unexpected happenings which seem to constantly topple. As soon as the individual is able to realize that on a Soul level he is his own partner, then he can experience a completely new shift in the ways others treat him. The difficulty before such understanding comes about is that others are always relating to the Uranian or impersonal part of him when he expects them to be relating to the personal part. Thus, there is a tremendous amount of forced Soul growth in this position as the individual is learning, perhaps after many lifetimes, to finally stand on his own.

The Retrograde Phase experienced will change constantly according to the nature of the person being related to, for there is constant effort as the individual tries to synchronize himself with others until he learns that he does not have to do this. He then develops an inner awareness of his cosmic relationships with everyone he comes into contact with.

RETROGRADE URANUS IN THE EIGHTH HOUSE

Here the individual experiences the changing of other people's values. Personal attachments to friends and lovers are difficult as the constant transmutation of ideals makes steady security difficult. While much awareness is received through the study of others, it is hard for the person to hold onto those who give him his information.

Unusual sexual experiences occur during the first half of life, ultimately serving as teaching tools to bring the individual into a higher sexual consciousness. Some with this position experience harrowing sexual encounters as well as periods of celibacy.

There is always a great depth of understanding relating to many different areas of life. This makes this person an interesting individual to others. But he has to learn how to express his ideas openly and tactfully. The Karma here is to appreciate the uniquely independent values of others so that the individual learns how to give others their own psychic space. In past lives he has undoubtedly experienced periods in which he was overly possessive. Even in the current life, this position levels off this tendency in the rest of the horoscope. The introspective qualities of the eighth house, along with some of the asexual tendencies of the Retrograde Uranus, sometimes produce a hermit-like existence. This allows the person to learn an enormous amount about his own sense of priorities.

The Retrograde Phases expressed here usually depend upon other people in the life as well as the sign on the eighth house cusp. Otherwise the individual experiences the Phase I tendencies of the Retrograde Uranus along with the Phase III qualities of the eighth house. Thus, the sign and the external factors in his life combine to make him vibrate to any particular phase during a given moment.

RETROGRADE URANUS IN THE NINTH HOUSE

Here the individual goes through an extremely unique adventure in consciousness. On one level he experiences Phase I of the Retrograde Process during which he anxiously assimilates new philosophies and spiritual awarenesses along with a desire to ingest all he can. There is a reaching for all that has worth to his higher being. At the same time, on a much deeper level, he is bringing a spiritual consciousness developed long ago into the present life. Thus, he may well be experiencing an abundance of holy knowledge from Biblical days in his past which creates in him a powerful desire to bring such understandings into his present.

His great awareness of life seems to be coming from a different source than the average norm, for the ways in which he expresses himself are always rather unique. He has a great love for the ideas of "God" but not for the official format of any specific religious tradition. Fighting against rules, he knows the inner rules which will do him the most good.

Sometimes he can lose his conscious train of thought because he is so interested in everything, that he has difficulty narrowing his field of focus. Karmically he is learning how to be spiritually, philosophically, religiously, and emotionally independent. He must develop his understanding of life regardless of what is socially acceptable to the rest of the world and be able to stand on what he knows works for him. Often this will lead him to experience much criticism from his friends and peers. In some cases it even causes breaks in marital ties. But still, his ultimate truth must come from his own unique sense of identity rather than from any need to compromise what he knows for the sake of personal accepta- bility.

RETROGRADE URANUS
IN THE TENTH HOUSE

Here the person seeks an inner sense of identity which affords him a uniqueness of character within the framework of the society he lives in. He experiences the conflict of com- promising his individuality in order to keep himself in a position from which he can ultimately express it more.

He may change his direction many times, until he finds that special niche where he truly is able to express himself. This is an especially excellent position for careers in advertis- ing and mass media communication through which the per- son can have his versatility along with the security he needs.

He has to have enough room to follow his creative in- stincts without being forced into the pressures of responsi- bility. Yet he handles responsibility beautifully when he is not aware that he is doing it! When he is allowed to live and work on a day-to-day basis he does much better than when he is confronted with any project which involves a great amount of long-range planning. Yet he is very capable at the de- velopment of long-range plans so long as he does not see them as boxing in his future.

Usually he spends much time in Phase III of the Retrograde Process assimilating the needs of his immediate envi- ronment and from this is able to understand how to cope with all that is around him. Still there is a tendency to be a little bit out of time synchronization, particularly as Uranus rules the future while the Saturnian tendencies of the tenth house relate more to qualities of the past. In blending the two, this individual has much work to do in gaining a balanced perspective in time. He is enormously inventive and usually can display rare genius in the understanding of how to do things that no one else around him can comprehend. Karmically he is learning lessons of self-discipline so that all of the inner inventiveness he feels can be put into use in the present world he lives in. He must learn how to be different without upsetting the structures he ultimately wishes to improve.

RETROGRADE URANUS IN THE ELEVENTH HOUSE

Here the individual is experiencing new awarenesses in areas of friendships, goals and ideals. There had been glimpses of these in the past, but now he is able to receive understanding on the deeper levels of his inner consciousness. He is a very original thinker, for his ideas are not bound by society's mundane reality. On the personal level, however, he tends to misinterpret friendships so that he ultimately has to review their meaning by changing his concepts later on. He attracts people from all walks of life so that he himself grows extremely colorful in his ideas, his dreams, and his personal outlook.

He finds that people don't always react the way he expected them to, and this teaches him how to respect the individuality of others. He grows detached and impersonal, but this helps him to gain illumination from the vantage point of objectivity. While he can rebel against all that holds people down, he really tries to stay out of interfering with their personal Karmic burdens. Being a crusader for fair play, he will rarely take sides in disputes since he is enlightened enough to see how meaningless they usually are in the first place.

When he comes across people who are blinded to themselves, he would like to be able to open their eyes to a higher consciousness. But, he will never force others to see things his way. Rather, he would hope that he could be of help to them, knowing that one of the rules of this world is that each man's growth must manifest at its own rate.

Karmically, he is experiencing a very enlightened sense of reality known only to himself, but through Phase I of the Retrograde Process he is able to project his illumination so that those who are capable of seeing can receive glimpses of an impersonal heightened state of awareness.

RETROGRADE URANUS
IN THE TWELFTH HOUSE

Here the individual experiences Phase III of the Retrograde Process during which he draws upon the awareness and understanding he had reached in former lifetimes as he sees the need for using them now. In some individuals this may indicate an understanding of Astrology in a former life. In others, where this is not the case, the Retrograde Uranus symbolizes major shifts in consciousness that happen within the individual. The potential for very real self-growth is very great.

If the individual's current life circumstances and behavior patterns point to it, along with confirmation from other areas in the horoscope, this Uranus placement can also be a past life indicator of some form of sexual abnormality or homosexuality. Still, no matter how it works on personal levels, this placement shows an inner ingenuity that comes through on higher channels of consciousness. This person knows how things work in the outer world and as a result does not always have to experience them all in action. His inner mind is experiencing everything all the time.

He is highly adaptable and will change his opinions because he is not possessive of ideas. Also, he does not try to constantly harmonize disharmonious thoughts. He has a great ability to let the Universe be, so that in return it will afford him the inner freedom he needs. While his changing values may seem at times to be quite eccentric, he is nevertheless unrestricted by the format of tradition which keeps most of society bound in its own chains. Still, he has to live in society, and healthy aspects to Saturn will enable him to put his Uranian awarenesses into a practical interplay between his knowledge and the world around him.

RETROGRADE NEPTUNE
ESOTERIC SYMBOL

Neptune's symbol (♆) is formed by the Crescent of Soul ascending from the Cross of Matter. The horizontal line of the Cross falls closer to the bottom of the figure, suggesting almost an inversion of the Cross symbol, as it seems to be falling away from the rising Crescent of Soul. Here, the formless lifts from the formed, as the Soul's sincere desire rises above the lesser importance of matter. Much like spiritual waters above the earth, the symbol represents the dissolving of matter that no longer needs to be crystallized.

It is interesting to note that the inverted Cross bespeaks of matter dropping away into lower worlds. This is in great measure descriptive of the mystical qualities of the planet.

When Neptune is Retrograde, the Cross appears upright through the inverted symbol, and the individual is more aware of his Soul as the Crescent of Soul appears closer to the earth plane. There develops a powerful inner need to approach all material things in the world in terms of their deepest significance to the Soul. In a sense then, the Retrograde Neptune may indeed give the individual the opportunity to express a very advanced stage of evolution, since it forces him to live in this world, but not be of it!

RETROGRADE NEPTUNE
PERSONALITY

The personality of the individual with Retrograde Neptune is not easily understood by others. His motives do not possess the common sense that one expects to be at the root of all motivation. Instead, he vibrates to a higher music, heard only to himself. His perceptions do not come from the material plane, but are a direct connection with his Soul. Thus, he can be highly spiritual but cares little for the formed side of orthodox religion. He can have a great love for music, but cannot ascribe to any definite man-made structure within it. He senses practically everything, but he relates his senses much less to physical reality than to his perception of a cosmic universe. He knows much more than he could ever put into words, for here again he realizes the limiting qualities of language as being but just another formed boundary which could encircle his infinite understanding. He is able to see the appearances and illusions that others live in, and therefore has to try to make the best bargain between not toppling their sand castles, while retaining all the inner truths he knows.

RETROGRADE NEPTUNE
KARMA

The individual with Retrograde Neptune is living through the Karma of learning how to sort out that which is real in terms of his ideals, and that which gives the appearance of fulfilling his dreams. He knows what he needs but has difficulty finding it in the external world. Constantly living one dream after another, he often winds up running from imaginary shadows, while chasing unrealistic fantasies. Still, he must find his ideals in the world of "no form" which has such a strong hold on him. He sometimes makes the mistake of projecting past dreams into present situations. This does not allow him to see the reality of the present clearly. He is highly intuitive, and through the different Retrograde Phases he is often able to know the outcome of situations long before he gets into them. But until he learns how to cope with the subtle flow of Neptunian energy that he feels within himself, he does not easily trust his intuition.

These individuals must learn how to integrate their senses with the ideals and dreams that they bring into this life. Instead of trying to distort perceptions in order to make the present fit the past, there must be an awarness of what parts of the present truly symbolize the parts of the past that are karmically incomplete.

RETROGRADE NEPTUNE
IN LEO

Here the individual often experiences illusions of grandeur. He lives in the appearance of glamour, glitter, and all the splendor of palatial illusion.

Spending much time in Phase I of the Retrograde Process, it is important for him to impress others. What he fails to realize is that this never quite brings him the satisfaction he is seeking, for he is just as easily impressed by others who are doing the same thing to him.

This placement of Neptune occurred during the great film era of Hollywood, when it was fashionable to identify with movie stars in an attempt to find more creative power in one's own self image. Homes were furnished with crystal chandeliers, velvet chairs, and many of the symbols of different movie sets.

On an individual basis, this Neptune placement leads a person to identify with power. At the very least, he needs to experience the appearance of achievement.

For his own self-growth he must raise his consciousness to the point that he sees this need in terms of his true spiritual goals rather than the symbols of beauty he is able to amass on the physical plane. Karmically, he is to take the enormous power of his positive belief systems, which he has come into this life with; get in touch with them, and then help to create the better world his Soul has dreamed of.

RETROGRADE NEPTUNE IN VIRGO

In this placement, Neptune is in its Astrological fall. Unable to experience the full freedom that it likes, the imaginative processes become focused on a world too small to allow full expression. The individual sees the whole by viewing all of its separate parts. While this makes it easier for him to crystallize his impressions, it puts him through many detailed steps that a more cosmically positioned Neptune would not need. However, he is able to combine the infinite imagination with the practicality of the real world, and as such can see the relationships between that which is within the realm of the five senses and that which is beyond. A great deal of clairvoyance is found in the Neptune in Virgo generation.

On a purely personal level, the Retrograde nature of the

planet tends to throw the individual back and forth between Phases I and III. He first perceives the future and then, as he is living it, realizes that he will spend much time later reflecting over his past. For this reason the Phase II experience is crucial in this placement as the personal touches both his future and his past while he is living in the world of outer experience. In fact it is his outer experiences that make his past and future come together in his inner reality. So long as he does not confuse his microcosmic view of the universe with what he macrocosmically understands, he can literally walk in two worlds at the same time.

Karmically he sees and knows that there is more to his world than what is immediately apparent. At the same time he understands that he must make his practical realistic bargain with the reality of his presence in day-to-day living. He does well when he can synchronize his intuition with what is practical and realistic, filtering out in the process all that is unimportant.

RETROGRADE NEPTUNE IN LIBRA

Here, Phase III of the Retrograde Process is experienced as the individual impersonally absorbs impressions from his environment. He usually thinks that all of the feelings he experiences are his own and that they ultimately demand some type of action or solution on his part. The truth is, however, that this placement gives the individual an opportunity to experience much of the universe while not truly being obligated to personalize it. He is highly sensitive, particularly to music and the arts, and has a great deal of difficulty dealing with the harshness in life, to which he is overly open. In order to balance himself he makes the mistake that he must balance all that is around him. This makes him tend to be interested in other people's business more than is actually good for him. He should understand that each new grain of sand he adds to Libra's scales as a balanced solution to what is already there creates still another imbalance demanding a new solution. Many with this configuration become so frustrated at trying to center the world around them that they eventually resort to drugs or other forms of escapism to keep from recognizing that their own personal difficulties are coming from problems which need no solutions.

When this configuration is correctly used, it gives the individual a tremendous amount of insight into the mirror of himself, or that part of his identity which he sees through the eyes of others. Karmically he can learn to integrate better with his society through this type of vision. At the same time he will be further removed from the basic essence of himself because he seeks to experience himself through others. He can reach happiness when he realizes that one does not reach for happiness but that it is found within as a more or less permanent state of contentment with one's individual life experience and the minute part one plays in the totality of the cosmic plan.

RETROGRADE NEPTUNE IN SCORPIO

This is a very special placement for the Retrograde Neptune. It adds subtlety and scope to the depth of the individual. The visionary qualities are increased along with an intuitive understanding of the unconscious. Able to function through all three Retrograde Phases, this person can gently transform himself as well as the world around him. He can be impersonally intense about his needs and the directions he feels the world is moving in, but at the same time, the Neptunian detachment and dissolving influence prevent him from being weighed down by his sensory impressions.

The generation with this placement is going to bring about a complete transformation in music, the arts, and medicine; bringing to the surface many overlooked qualities that only their keen awareness is capable of finding.

Unless one experiences it personally, it becomes difficult to imagine the tremendous depth that is possible when the introspective nature of the Retrograde brings the subtle unconscious of Neptune in full touch with Scorpio's Plutonian power for change.

Individuals with this placement will be at their greatest strength during mid-life as they fulfill their Karma of gently helping the world to end the Piscean Age. This will be done by replacing all that was dying with the new spiritual consciousness that only they are capable of understanding at its true depth. The person with Retrograde Neptune in Scorpio is one who, on an individual basis, dissolves the past. He is a forerunner of the Future — reshaping the formless for the needs of meaningful growth.

RETROGRADE NEPTUNE IN SAGITTARIUS

Here, the individual experiences a heightened consciousness of the world and his place in it. He learns to live without anchoring himself to roots. Instead, he lives a more natural existence, flowing with the currents of his fortune.

He is a free spirit with very few attachments that are meaningful to him on the physical plane. With almost a prophetic insight into the future, he can grasp the essence of things in a moment, but he has difficulty stabilizing himself in every day practical matters. He will play a great role in delivering the spiritual message of the Aquarian Age. His life is built on the expansion of formless horizons he senses within himself. At the same time, he is an endless giver of information and knowledge to others. Through Phase I of the Retrograde Process he can perceive distant possibilities as very real probabilities in the here and now. He is a dreamer of the first order. But his dreams are more of a vision for mankind rather than fulfillment of personal desires.

More than with other placements, this gives a powerful sense of the cosmic whole happening within oneself. Bursting with life, this person is a pure expression of the Soul finally set free.

Karmically, he is not to be bound by anything other than what he perceives as the deepest truths within himself. He will avoid mass movements, organizations, clubs, the institution of marriage, and any other man-made structure which prevents him from experiencing all that he feels inside.

RETROGRADE NEPTUNE IN THE FIRST HOUSE

This individual constantly lives in a state of illusion. Spending much time in Phase I of the Retrograde Process, he continually imagines himself in different identities as he keeps trying to displace a constant feeling of loneliness. Much of his life is on the unconscious level as he keeps sifting through his formless nature trying to establish a concrete sense of belonging to himself. Like a chameleon, he is in a constant state of change, always readjusting himself to the environment he is in at the moment.

Most people with this placement have a tendency to feel sorry for themselves, always believing that something is missing in them that might be found in another person. This feeling can be overcome as soon as the person accepts the formless part of himself as his true nature, understanding that this gives him the freedom to blend with his environment so that his true identity is more cosmic than personal.

At some point in a former life he began to imagine himself as different than his ideas of himself. And whether he knew it or not, that was the beginning of his spiritual journey. In this life he will continue to sacrifice old parts of his identity until he truly blends with his higher cosmic nature. He will learn that all of life is but appearance, including the image he believes he has of himself.

RETROGRADE NEPTUNE IN THE SECOND HOUSE

Here the formless nature of Neptune presents a natural conflict with the form structure of the second house. The individual has difficulty crystalizing his value systems, and tends to be indecisive. He can be overly generous during Phase I while feeling that he has to guard against losing things during Phase III.

From past incarnations, he has learned to value the arts and he usually has a good sense of appreciation for music, but the Retrograde nature of Neptune does not allow him to pursue these as much as he would like. Should they occur as influences in his life, he would be very happy, but the drive nature to seek them must come from somewhere else in the horoscope.

Neptune is at a strong disadvantage in the second house, because it keeps dissolving all the individual tries to acquire. His financial security is nebulous. So are the values he stands for. Every time he tries to be firm he grows more pliable.

During his early years, he can be particularly sensitive and sometimes even gullible. But as he grows, much of this changes into a truly compassionate and soft nature.

Although he willl have much difficulty standing up for what he believes is right, this is only part of his Karma. He is living this incarnation in order to dissolve any false values within him that he has brought forward from the past.

RETROGRADE NEPTUNE IN THE THIRD HOUSE

With this placement the individual experiences all three Retrograde Phases. He tries to be in tune with whoever he is communicating with, but often has difficulty coming to the point. He can beat around the bush, taking his listener in circles before saying what he knew he wanted to say right from the beginning.

In many instances there was a great deal of past life sorrow in relationships which the individual is unconsciously trying to forget. This gives him difficulty in expressing confidence in his current life relationships. He is easy to please, but finds it difficult to believe he is really capable of pleasing others. Often, he goes far out of his way trying to gain acceptance.

He can be highly psychic, but until he develops more confidence in himself, this gift can be more of a hindrance to him than a help. If his lack of confidence leads him to be a negative thinker, then most of his psychic impressions will be on the negative and somber side. But, once he overcomes his own negativity, the higher rays of Neptune give him a very clear and beautiful insight into the people he would like to relate with.

Since he is unusually sensitive to others he must teach himself to believe in the positive qualities of those around him. The moment he can do this, his life changes dramatically for the better.

He is living through a Karma of learning an unusually subtle and well-evolved form of communication that will ultimately bring him to understandings that language cannot express.

RETROGRADE NEPTUNE IN THE FOURTH HOUSE

Here the individual experiences a great deal of disillusionment in his family placement. He has difficulty identifying with family role structures all through his life, because he is ultimately to base his foundation on a more cosmic reality. When he tries to be personally possessive of the past, it seems to elude him. The anchors in life that one normally tries to hold onto are not really afforded him. Thus, he must find another, more universal, reality in which his foundation is built on intangibles rather than the solidity of things and clutching relationships.

Until he learns this, however, he spends most of his time in Phase III of the Retrograde Process, bemoaning all the sorrow he feels at watching his roots dissolve from under his feet. Often, he wishes he could go back to the past and build that which never was. But, Karmically, he must come to learn that his Soul never really had the need for the kind of solid foundation he sees in others.

When he realizes this, he experiences a losing of the "little self" (or as psychologists say — "the child") in order to make room for the more cosmically-tuned adult. This is a difficult position for marriage because each year there is more and more need for being less dependent. As the desire for emotional security lessens, this individual can rise to great spiritual heights if he learns how to put his creative imagination in the right direction.

RETROGRADE NEPTUNE IN THE FIFTH HOUSE

Here much time is spent in Phase I of the Retrograde Process in which the individual initiates his life by creating through his dreams. Being highly intuitive, he has the ability to see his own creations so long as he does not delude himself about reality. Sometimes there is a tendency to create his own reality in place of that which the world around him is living in. Then he tries to project this outwardly, fitting each person he meets to characters that can fulfill the roles in his self-created play.

At the same time, he responds to a very subtle yet beautiful creative instinct. He can be musically or artistically talented, but he has to learn to combine effort to make his inspirations his reality.

In many ways he listens to a different drummer and will often go astray before accepting the confines of the society he lives in. He always wants a personal dream to identify with which would make him different from the mundane world he sees. Usually his religious beliefs are quite different from the principles of any established orthodox religion. There is a great deal of sensuality with this placement. This is another manifestation of the individual's inner sense of Neptunian freedom of expression of his unconscious creative impulses.

Karmically his life revolves around learning to believe inwardly that which he wishes others to believe outwardly. Thus, in all ways that he can express or impress himself, he will do whatever he has to do in order to establish and then build on a belief system which was too weak in prior lifetimes.

RETROGRADE NEPTUNE
IN THE SIXTH HOUSE

This is the true Angel of Mercy. Here the dissolving qualities of the Retrograde Neptune are offered to others as a mission of healing, service, and great personal sacrifice. Many in the medical and nursing professions, as well as faith healers, are blessed with this placement.

Usually expressed in Phase I of the Retrograde Process, the individual seeks opportunities and situations where he will be needed. Most of his dreams and ambitions are dedicated to how he can creatively serve the society that has given him so much in the past. Truly, this is one of Neptune's special positions, for it allows all those who have it to bring their cosmic understanding down to the earth plane where it can be of practial use to others. In this house, Neptune is in its Astrological fall, describing exactly how difficult this is to do personally. But, Neptune is not a personal planet. As long as the individual can be a servant without being a slave, he will try his best to live the life of a very dedicated humanitarian.

Karmically, he is living a life of service, and the more he serves, the more he frees himself from the wheel of Karma.

RETROGRADE NEPTUNE
IN THE SEVENTH HOUSE

This placement forces the individual to become highly independent. The promised strength of others is denied, either through the escapism of a marriage partner or the unreality of other people in the individual's life. He learns how to trust and depend upon himself. The Retrograde Phase which is accentuated will naturally depend upon which sign is on the seventh house cusp, but it will also depend highly upon the individual's mate.

Usually the individual reacts as a kind of secondary response to the way this planet is being used by those he loves. Through a tremendous sensitivity to other people's feelings, he grows more compassionate as the years pass. He learns to expect less from those who are less able to give. And, he learns how to build more within himself.

He is living through a very spiritual Karma of experiencing impersonal love in that one area of his life where he consciously expected personal love. While he will go through some disappointments in his intimate relationships, he is blessed with a tremendous opportunity for Soul growth through sincere sacrifice.

He will have to draw on much strength from within himself, because in this incarnation he will experience a good deal of loneliness. And much of the love he expects to receive from others will in actuality be the exact mirror of what he himself gives out. Thus, it is less the love from others that he feels than how much they show him the amount of love he is giving. If married, he will pay a Karmic debt to his partner through sacrificial love.

RETROGRADE NEPTUNE
IN THE EIGHTH HOUSE

This is a very strong position for the Retrograde Neptune, giving the individual keen insight into the values of others. He likes to serve, and is highly conscius of the needs of others. At the same time, the Retrograde nature of the planet tends to make him hold back. He keeps his impressions to himelf, often seeming to be in a state of suspended animation, until he senses the need for his service. There is a great deal of semi-conscious sexual visualization here, based on what the person feels he needs from life. Still, in this area and in the world of business and finance, he needs direction to keep him from confusing himself. The Retrograde nature of Neptune combined with the inward tendencies of the eighth house, makes him highly introspective as he spends most of his time in Phase III of the Retrograde Process.

One of the most unique characteristics of this placement is that the individual is born with natural mediumistic talents, which if properly developed can lead to a very enriched life of continual cosmic realization.

RETROGRADE NEPTUNE IN THE NINTH HOUSE

Here the Retrograde Neptune finds a special place in which its intuitive powers exhalt the understanding of the higher mind. If positively aspected the depth of inspiration can be enormous. The individual is capable of grasping the higher essence of life and its true meaning. Often he experiences rejection and a sense of loneliness in his personal relationships, but this only serves to make him more cosmically aware of his Divine nature.

He is overly sensitive to his environment, tending at times to exaggerate his sensory impressions. His moods are strongly influenced by weather conditions, and the general harmonic vibrations of wherever he is at any given moment. Being a very compassionate soul, he can direct his senses purposefully if he feels he is serving some higher calling.

It is during Phase I of the Retrograde Process where the visionary qualities of this placement become outstanding. Karmically the individual is destined to understand himself on his most subtle levels. Temporary withdrawals from society help him to see his higher essence more clearly. In this life he is continuing a search for truth through following the order of nature and natural cosmic law.

RETROGRADE NEPTUNE
IN THE TENTH HOUSE

Here, the Retrograde Neptune finds itself in a difficult placement. The individual's personal need for direction in life is continually dissolved by the formlessness of the cosmic reality he reaches. He often feels confused about his goals because he senses the infinite plan of the world and has difficulty comparing anything he could do against it. As such, he can have tremendous insight but his drive is weakened by the non-competitive nature of his being.

He can be highly creative and should be engaged in an occupation in which inspirational and visionary qualities are needed. If the sign on the cusp of the Tenth House is negative, than the individual spends much time in Phase III of the Retrograde Process in which he not only absorbs the ideals of his peers, but also tends to be shy when confronted with public or social situations.

He is working through a Karma of learning how to be not only impersonal in his career, but also not to identify with status or social position. Once he learns this, he can be keenly intuitive and highly prophetic, experiencing much social success, because he is not desiring it. Perhaps, the simplest way of reaching his true understanding of his feelings is when he realizes that he who wins the "rat race" has merely proven he is the biggest rat!

RETROGRADE NEPTUNE
IN THE ELEVENTH HOUSE

Here the individual tends to withdraw from the creative process. He spends most of his time in Phase III, retreating into a dream world that has become his reality. He tends to be on the impractical side, as the scope of his imagination far surpasses the reality of the world around him. He is highly compassionate and will often sacrifice much for the needs of others. He is so deeply appreciative of life itself that creating things for himself is far less important to him than just experiencing the essence of all he can absorb.

He likes to feel needed by his friends for he gets much deep meaning from them.

With this position the individual brings into this life a Karma built on past dreams. This usually makes him idealistic to the point that he does not easily discipline himself to the standards of society. He alwasy feels that there is a higher music, a more subtle meaning to life, and a deeper understanding of what the the world calls love. Of all the Zodiacal placements this is the one individual who can give generously, not only without expecting something in return, but not even wanting the other person to know that he was the giver.

The level of awareness can be unusually high, as the traditions and restrictions of society do not bind the individual's creative imagination. A dreamer in past lives, a seeker of Uranian awareness in this life, he must learn how to balance all he intuitively feels with all he must deal with on more mundane and practical levels. Thus, it is not enough for him to imagine something idealistically wonderful. He must find the ways through other areas in his chart to impress his dreams into his creative reality.

RETROGRADE NEPTUNE
IN THE TWELFTH HOUSE

Here, in its natural home, the Retrograde Neptune gives great insight into the full cosmic reality. The individual is able to see the whole of things without having to dissect them. His vision is detached and impersonal because he can easily dissolve past Karma by not holding opinions of it.

Many with this position are capable of mediumship as they can understand the essence of things without getting personally involved. The past gets dissolved easily as the individual instinctively knows it has no basis in reality.

During the first half of life, the lesser cosmic attributes of the Retrograde Neptune are more pronounced. The individual experiences an inner sorrow that makes him a kind of collective psychic garbage pail for everyone he comes into contact with. But once he begins to sense the true essence of things, much of his own self-pity becomes replaced by a greater tolerance for the universe in which he lives.

There is a strong tendency to experience Phase III of the

Retrograde Process as he goes back over the pictures of all he has already been through, in a more subtle reality, so that all that he does not need to carry with him into the future becomes loosened.

Nearly always, this position gives the individual the ability to attune himself to his true cosmic identity.

RETROGRADE PLUTO
ESOTERIC SYMBOL

In the symbol of Pluto (♇) we find the Circle of Spirit soaring free above the connection between the Crescent of Soul and the Cross of Matter. This is so indicative of the unknown areas man has to pass through before finally reaching an understanding of himself at the very deepest of levels.

When the Soul and the Matter part of existence are not in contact with the essential Spirit of Light, the individual experiences the baser Plutonian energies. But, when he begins to transcend the unknown quantities within himself, he is able to bridge the gap between his lower life and finally link up with the Spirit of purified Golden Light that God had intended him to know. When man is able to achieve this, he comes into contact with that part of himself that is so essentially good that he is sure that no one he knows would actually believe it. This is his real identity.

The great difficulties involved in reaching such Plutonian energies, is that like the seagull who flies the highest on his own wings, each individual must transcend himself on his own. The endings qualified by Pluto are the symbolic dropping off of phases no longer necessary for the individual's growth.

Since Pluto is Retrograde nearly half of the time, then a very high percentage of the world's population has this configuration appearing in their natal horoscopes. These individuals will ultimately become more concerned with transformations within themselves than with less fruitful attempts at trying to reform the outer world. By inverting the symbol, all else rises from the manifestation of the Divine Spirit expressing itself here on earth.

RETROGRADE PLUTO
PERSONALITY

This individual with Retrograde Pluto feels the ills of society as a personal reason to transform himself. He knows that he cannot change the world. Still, he would like to if it were practical or possible. But, he can change the world within himself by ending his ties with all that bind him to less than his purified being. This is a process that takes many years, and sometimes many lifetimes to achieve. In its highest manifestation it represents the true Christ Consciousness of bringing the purest form of love here to earth.

In lesser measure and more common, he is continually eliminating from his life all those factors which impede the progress of his Soul and the expression of his Spirit.

The individual with Retrograde Pluto experiences the struggle of mankind as a very personal struggle within himself. He personally feels the need to overcome in himself all that has been lowering the consciousness of the society he lives in. Thus, he reacts strongly to other people's dishonesty to themselves; taking it as a personal affront to his own progress, which he feels he must make for the ultimate good of the civilization of which he is an important part. He must learn to detach a little more from the habit patterns and behavior characteristics of others whose lives really have so little to do with his own true inner reality.

RETROGRADE PLUTO
KARMA

The individual with Retrograde Pluto is living through a Karma of experiencing mass consciousness within himself. He feels the impact of world thought, and is conscious of how it relates to world thought throughout the ages. Not always expressing outwardly what he knows, he tends to see other individuals as part of a larger and more inclusive whole rather than on a constant one-to-one basis.

In his personal life, it is far less important what he does than what he thinks about what he does. Much of the time he lives within his conscience, sifting through the great multitude of feelings he experiences within himself.

The spiritual growth possible with Retrograde Pluto is limited only by the individual's conscious mind. He can literally rise above much of the Karma of his entire race if he chooses. Interestingly enough, if he tries to avoid elevating his Karma, he will feel the lower Karmas of others around him anyway. Thus, if he chooses to elevate himself, he truly can begin to live Jesus's parable of "being in this world but not of it." In order to eventually achieve this he goes through temporary withdrawals during the first half of life, until he learns how to be impersonal with the intensity of the world he senses outside himself, so that he ultimately reaches the point at which he no longer feels it acting within himself.

RETROGRADE PLUTO IN CANCER

With this placement much time is spent in Phase III of the Retrograde Process as the individual keeps dealing with upheavals in his past. He spends his entire life trying to create a rebirth in his sytem of memory so that he can unlock from his consciousness all that had previously shaken him on an emotional level. Unfortunately this position has a tendency to fix the individual right at his trauma points. Thus, each new person or circumstance in his future is only symbolic of a past he has not left behind. The more effort he exerts killing the past, or even hiding it from himself, the more he focuses himself back in it. The more understanding he seeks to create within himself, the more he is drawn like a magnet back into the reasons which made him seek understanding in the first place. Thus he is on a treadmill until he learns that the power of memories dies in time if it is not constantly negatively powered.

Interestingly enough, many with this placement have experienced long continued trauma with either one or both parents and family crises never seem to end. The individual, while constantly trying to put an end to all that bothers him, never really vibrates away from the source of his difficulties. The entire Pluto in Cancer generation was emotionally traumatized because of world conditions at the time. Wars across the continents, the destruction caused by Adolf Hitler, and the subsequent breakup of families left very little for these individuals to be emotionally sure of. As a generation they are silently huddled together in fear; on an individual basis they tend strongly to thought project their unconscious dependencies to all who are around them. There is much inner suffering with this placement, which is perhaps the reason why those individuals with this Retrograde Pluto who internalize and personalize the full consciousness of their age group, try to find substitute security in the other world of material possessions.

Of course the key to ending the suffering of past unpleasant memories is not to regenerate them by seeking reminder symbols, but rather to view each day as a new birth of freshness.

RETROGRADE PLUTO
IN LEO

This configuration speaks of the overthrow of power for the purpose of transformation. On a worldwide basis, the Pluto in Leo generation came into a world weakened by its emotional dependencies, deluded by substitute materialism, and clinging to past values which were no longer serving a useful purpose. In the light of this, the new generation had not been scattered by a war-torn world, but was raised in the consciousness of a reconstruction period in which stress was put on the individual's ability to develop the strength within himself so that he (as part of a generation) could overcome oppression. Thus, we find the Pluto in Leo individual questioning the validity of the "establishment." He realizes that a million weak people belonging to any idea or organization which appears to give strength, may not only be a facade, but the entire creative construct may well be based on false values.

Through his Leonian desire for a world he can be proud to live in, he is perfectly willing to tear apart all that was built before him on foundations which he does not see as meaningful.

The Retrograde nature of the planet causes the individual to see this world shift in values as a personal crusade in which he is to play some intrinsic part. On a personal basis, he questions his identity in terms of what he himself is doing to make his world more meaningful. Thus, much time is spent in Phase I of the Retrograde Process as he tries to project a sense of secure strength built on honest foundations to a world that so sorely needs it.

He feels on a Karmic level the obligation to overcome all that has ever made mankind weak. Thus he spends his entire life with one goal in mind: to develop power first over himself, and then by example, over the false structures in society that need more creative and honorable foundations.

RETROGRADE PLUTO
IN VIRGO

With this placement the world entered the age of analysis. Mass consciousness began seeking to understand the mechanism that was creating its defects. Psychoanalysis became fashionable and literally thousands of new inroads into the human mind began to be explored. A compartmentalizing effect pervaded the world as man tried to sort out all that was making the world the way it was.

In an individual's chart this placement helps the powers of inner concentration. The person is able to focus his unconscious so that he can be a veritable dynamo in those specific areas in which he directs his attention. At the same time the Retrograde nature of the planet causes a desire for non-interference from outside sources. The person actually draws enjoyment out of working things out for himself.

In the end it is he who has solved his own riddles and knowing this makes them worth solving. In consciousness the individual experiences Phase I of the Retrograde Process. In his active life experience, his personal shyness with people is the classic expression of Phase III.

Karmically he is seeking to understand how things work. His approach to life seems a bit mechanical but it is the way he reaches his clearest understandings.

RETROGRADE PLUTO
IN LIBRA

Individuals with this placement have a rather unique

experience in consciousness. They are observers in the evolution and transformation of the world, but do not really experience the desire to be an intrinsic part of it. On one hand, they personally experience the consciousness of everyone around them. This makes them a curious blend of all they have seen or touched. On the other hand they don't relate to themselves personally. Thus, they do not stand for that which they appear to stand for. The result is that this placement acts as a window through which the race's consciousness passes.

A strong sense of responsibility for others gives many with this configuration a silent martyr complex. They feel that their ability to balance those around them reflects in their personal accounting to their God.

This is one of the most difficult positions for the Retrograde Pluto as the force of change disrupts Libra's state of gentle inertia. There is a drive towards accomplishment coupled to a desire not to participate. When Pluto entered Libra, many great "Guru movements" gained in popularity. Even the strong advent of transcendental meditation is a peculiar application of this placement. To transcend is the force of Pluto; to do this through meditation represents the quiet non-activity of Libra.

On an individual basis, the Retrograde action of the planet gives a person the ability to internalize human consciousness, so that he can become blended into the whole of all he perceives. This makes him go through Phase III of the Retrograde Process much of the time.

Karmically, those born with this placement have an internally quiet and impersonal desire to transform the age in which they live. Their goal is a more peaceful and harmonious state of consciousness.

RETROGRADE PLUTO
IN SCORPIO

In Scorpio, Pluto finds its natural home. Here the long awaited spiritual transformation of the world finally comes to pass. Great upheavals topple much of mankind's earlier creations as the closing of the Piscean Age begins to become more apparent. New scientific discoveries in the areas of the laws of physics, principles of medicine and ways of natural healing gain increasing acceptance. The world becomes increasingly divided as the struggle between "good" and "evil" surfaces in mass proportion. Giant social and political movements, whose seeds were sown earlier, begin to emerge with enormous power.

When Pluto is Retrograde the significance of these sweeping radical changes becomes intimately felt on the personal level. The eons of searching for an understanding of man's sexuality, his search to find his God (and the possible connection between these two drives) becomes a purely personal quest for each individual.

For those born with this Plutonian placement, there is a powerful desire to transcend all past failures by bringing to the surface and then eliminating all the hidden causes of weakness.

Man literally destroys himself in order to be reborn. This is one of the most tumultous periods in human history, as the Bible itself becomes deeply questioned as a prelude to a new Third Testament yet to be written. Fanaticism is prevalent everywhere, as a world tired from two thousand years of human suffering begins to shake itself loose in preparation for the Aquarian Age.

The individuals with Pluto Regrograde will be very much a part of these sweeping transformations, helping to stimulate (through Phase I of the Retrograde Process) Man's rebirth: out of his state of sleep and into a higher, wakeful consciousness.

RETROGRADE PLUTO
IN THE FIRST HOUSE

This is an extremely dynamic position for Pluto which puts the individual on a life-long quest to purify himself. He experiences constant transformations as his constant urge to seek brings him through many intense experiences. During youth he is highly impulisve, as he acts out Phase I of the Retrograde Process. After mid-life he becomes more introspective. Then, instead of wanting to impress himself on the world, he seeks to understand how much he is a product of the universe he lives in.

In all he does there is a powerful inner drive that motivates him. He is rarely content and extremely difficult to please for what he is seeking is usually beyond the grasp of those who try to help him. With Retrograde Pluto in the First House marriage and other relationships are difficult, as the inner turmoil of the individual makes his continual attempt to uproot and transform his needs and basic desires. He will spend most of the current incarnation transforming his personal concepts and learning to transcend the Karma of his personal identification as he uncovers the Cosmic reality. His anxiousness to achieve this is the reason why he lives so much in Phase I; but his true evolution always comes from the after-the-fact realizations he makes in Phase III.

RETROGRADE PLUTO
IN THE SECOND HOUSE

Here the individual is living through a Karma of bondage. Either he is chained to society's values or his own prior life's obsessive thoughts which must be brought to the surface in order to be eliminated. It doesn't really matter what binds him. What is important is his reaching the understanding that he must literally destroy his past value systems if he is ever to reach happiness. During the first half of life he does not see the world clearly. He tends to blame external factors for depriving him of all he thinks he needs. He must learn the difference between his wants and his needs, for although he may rarely get what he wants he will always have exactly what he needs.

In his personal life he can get highly possessive, unbelievably stubborn, and amazingly resistant to any external encouragement which tries to get him to fit in with the world around him. He would rather see the world bend to fit his ideals. As a result he lives in his self-created bonds, silently scorning all who disagree with his ideas.

This placement can denote a strong past-life residue of the animal self being brought into this incarnation to be overcome. In order to transform himself, this individual must carefully study his inner motives during Phase III of the Retrograde Process and realize that most of what he is holding onto and seeking has little basis in the reality of what truly makes him happy in the current life.

RETROGRADE PLUTO
IN THE THIRD HOUSE

Here all three Phases of the Retrograde Process play an important role in the individual's life. In areas of relationships, he tends to live his life backwards. First, he considers the end results. He then keeps trying to express himself in ways which will achieve the results before laying the necessary groundwork at the beginning. He later tries to retrace his steps, picking up the pieces he missed. His scope is very wide and he is highly sensitive to other people's unconscious thoughts. This causes him much pain because he often sees through the masks that people wear. As a result he finds it difficult to fully trust people because he senses their ulterior and perhaps unconscious motives.

This is an unusually psychic position and the individual is fully capable of communicating intimately with people he knows for just a few minutes. This helps him to see the truth if he is able to interpret his perceptions impersonally.

Karmically, he is being asked to master his senses. This may well be one of the most difficult lessons in all the Zodiac.

In his youth, he is highly sensitive to his environment. As he grows older he comes to realize that he only perceives what he focuses on. As a result he must work hard on transforming his attitudes toward the world around him, for he is literally in full control of the level of consciousness he will live at. He does best when he realizes that no thought he could ever think would be his own. Even his ideas of transforming others were never truly his own, but only other people's unconscious thoughts of themselves which he was sensitive enough to pick up. He can be a very powerful communicator and highly influential in changing world thought once he becomes impersonally oriented.

RETROGRADE PLUTO
IN THE FOURTH HOUSE

With this position the individual spends much time in

Phase III of the Retrograde Process in which he tends to shy away from outwardly expressing himself in a world which feels foreign to him. Often many childhood fears and phobias accompany this position. These manifest themselves as strong emotional dependencies. He strongly dislikes this aspect of himself and keeps trying to destroy all that gives him enough security to rob him of a sense of growth. This built-in conflict can cause a good deal of paranoid feelings as the individual projects his own self-destructive impulses onto others.

Truly he is experiencing a complete transformation of his Soul, so that at his very roots a new flower can be born. This means he will spend much effort in breaking all old habits, particularly those which create comfort that keeps pulling him back into his past. As a reslt he never feels fully sure of where he is. It is almost as if the ground he stands on keeps changing beneath him. In reality he is constantly rejecting the old while still fearful of the new. Yet he knows that forward is the only direction he can go. For many years life seems to be like running back and forth across a bridge, not willing to touch either shore for fear of losing the possibilities of experiencing the other. This position of Pluto indicates that the Soul has reached the end of a long behavior pattern it has been stuck in for many lifetimes. In this life, a new birth from within is finally to be effected.

RETROGRADE PLUTO
IN THE FIFTH HOUSE

Here the individual spends much time in Phase I of the Retrograde Process. He tries to express himself outwardly in order to prove to himself that the world will one day accept him. He can be forceful and dynamic. He has a powerful sexual nature. His geneal outlook on life, along with his drive can be overbearing. Being too subjective in his general outlook on life he must learn to be more conscious of other people's feelings. Until he can do this, he can distort his perceptions since the world is really more impersonal than he would like to believe.

With this placement there is sometimes one child that is

either difficult to raise or hard to reach in terms of the child's own personal sense of individuality. Usually the child refuses to be molded easily.In some cases the child tries to be the parent's teacher.

The love nature of the Fifth House Retrograde Pluto creates much inner turmoil as the individual is constantly questioning the different roles in which he sees himself. He may resent himself on very deep levels and is truly trying to find reasons for accepting himself and the society he lives in. This often takes the form of actively crusading for some form of personal expression that society in general does not readily approve of. In this manner he feels he is able to prove himself worthy of his own personal existence. He will reach happiness when he stops trying to topple the world and accepts himself as just one part in it.

Nearly always there is Karma relating to past-life misuse of the creative process. Often this has occurred in sexually-rooted thought projections. Now the individual must learn how to give free psychic space to those around him. As he learns to do this he will find himself with an abundance of new energy to be directed into new areas of creation and accomplishment.

RETROGRADE PLUTO
IN THE SIXTH HOUSE

Here the individual experiences great upheavals in his working conditions, his relations with superiors and his general give-and-take sense of obligation with the world. He goes through strange illnesses which often disappear just as mysteriously as they arise. He must learn not to personalize a sense of mission in life, for if he does, he becomes universally personal in the most negative sense. He can actually absorb all of society's ills unconsciously if he does so. This occurs because of his unconscious desire to transform the world so that it can conform to his own personal ideas of perfection.

He is living through a Karma of impersonal service in which all of his actions relate less to his individual identity than to his role in the cosmic plan. As such he functions best as a universal missionary, Until he learns this, he tends to experience some bitterness towards the world which is apparently cheating him out of all he is due. When he becomes introspective during Phase III of the Retrograde Process he actually hurts himself by going into himself and finding the world and its problems there instead of the identity he is seeking. This happens because he is so busy constantly getting into all that is around him which he later confuses with the pure essence of himself.

He reaches happiness when he stops trying to "see where the feet grow" and starts walking on them instead. In fact his whole life is dedicated to use, coming from instinctive understanding rather than trying to make unconscious understanding conscious.

RETROGRADE PLUTO
IN THE SEVENTH HOUSE

Here the individual experiences great obstacles to overcome in his relations with others. In marriage he may tend to unconsciously disrupt the harmony he thinks he is seeking. Spending much of his energy trying to reform others, he does not always clearly look at himself. In this position all three Retrograde Phases are experienced because so much depends upon who the individual is relating to at any given moment. In all people there are at least two different major conceptions of the Self. One is based on what one thinks of oneself. The other is based upon what a person thinks others think about him. It is this second Self that the individual with Retrograde Pluto in the Seventh House is karmically working on transforming. As a result the environment he moves in controls him more than he realizes. Constantly absorbing the external consciousness of his outer life, he is a curious blend of all society thinks at any given time along with a strong unconscious hostility in the first or original Self for not being able to truly express its own (non-society influenced) nature. Therefore, this is an extremely difficult position for marriage because any intimate relationship merely heightens this struggle between fitting into some niche and secretly wanting to destroy all in the world that creates these niches. A great transormation is realized at the discovery of the true basis of his reality. The fact is, that the society he lives in, with all the complaints he has about it, including the institutions it set up which bind him, are exactly the very things he needs to make him vibrate to the essence of life itself.

RETROGRADE PLUTO
IN THE EIGHTH HOUSE

This is unquestionably the position with the most depth in the entire Zodiac. Not only does Pluto rule the Eighth House but the introspective qualities of its Retrograde nature are in total harmony with its house placement. Here the individual is constantly questioning the values of others. He seeks to understand the deepest mysteries. To him sexuality represents the most unfathomable question of all. Little in life goes by him without his clinically studying it. He has a very strong sexual nature. His drive, however, is not only physical, but mental and cosmically oriented as well. Whether he expresses it physically or transforms it to mental regions this drive is powering all he seeks to understand in the universe. Usually expressed during Phase I of the Retrograde Process, this position aggressively creates constant destruction in old traditional habit patterns so that ultimately the individual can go through a rebirth within himself on the very deepest of levels.

He is so linked with the values of others, that whether he likes it or not, he is strongly influenced by mass consciousness. He brings into this life a legacy of Pluto's power for change, and the more he grows discontented with the world around him, the more he begins to fathom the myseries within himself.

RETROGRADE PLUTO
IN THE NINTH HOUSE

Here the individual experiences Phase I of the Retrograde Process as he seeks to explore all he perceives in the unverse. This makes him rather difficult to understand by others who are more rooted in the day-to-day mundane world of practical reality. Whether he is aware of it or not, he tends towards astral projection from one place to another, and from one realm in consciousness to another on an almost constant basis.

Of all the placements in the Zodiac, this is the one in which the individual's consciousness is the least connected to his physical body. He is constantly attracted to world thought, and much of his own personal thoughts have less to do with his own life than with the universe he is unconsciously exploring at any given moment.

He is a rebel against restrictions; seeing the world as a playground for his Soul to exercise and grow in. He has the ability to understand so much that he must learn how to focus himself to one thought, or one project at a time.

There is great wisdom in this position as soon as the individual learns that he is allowed to walk with his head in the clouds so long as his feet are on the ground. Because he sees so much, he eventually becomes very sure of his opinons and attitudes which can cause him much difficulty in relating to others who do not fully understand his sources of information.

Karmically, he is learning how to cope with the full essence of thought streams which are unbounded by individual possessiveness. He is one of the few people in the Zodiac who really knows that a person is not what he thinks. If used correctly, and with proper training, this can be an extremely spiritual placement for the Retrograde Pluto.

RETROGRADE PLUTO
IN THE TENTH HOUSE

With this position the individual experiences a great inner drive to establish a substantial identity among his peers. He usually needs a career. The idea of any mundane job is too unfulfilling for the demands of Pluto's dynamic energy.

This is one of the few positions in which desire stemming from the unconscious does not necessarily manifest itself on a sexual level. The individual is too concerned with feeling that he must justify his sense of self-worth to allow his energies to dissipate in any areas other than those which directly relate to the goals he has set for himself. Many with this placement seek work in which they feel they are helping to transform or enlighten the public, thus fulfilling themselves to the extent that they are fulfilling the world they live in.

There is a strong sense of responsibility but not always to the traditional. If anything, this person wants to break the shackles of society so that he can be part of something new which will eventually take its place. He vascillates between Phase I and Phase III of the Retrograde Process as he compares all that the world could be with all he has seen it was in the past. Personally, he identifies with great causes and great downfalls and is at his happiest when he feels he is a part of some great world transformation.

He is living through the Karma of learning how to constructively direct power for the best possible good of the society he lives in.

RETROGRADE PLUTO
IN THE ELEVENTH HOUSE

Here Pluto finds its most idealistic position as the individual wants the best for himself, his friends, and the world he lives in. Usually, this causes much havoc for he sees a great gap between his ideal nature and the way things really are. Thus, he can appear as a rebel trying to close this gap by literally destroying all that he sees as totally meaningless. Often, he appoints himself as the conscience of his friends. This, while it is motivated by a highly spiritual desire, often causes great friction. Much of life is seen from the point of view of a spectator and the creative process can be hampered as the individual questions the meaning of things perhaps even more than he personally participates in them. He takes his friendships quite seriously and personally identifies with their successes and failures. This placement usually manifests Phase III of the Retrograde Process in which an internalization of past consciousness motivates the individual to the point where he can inspire others so that through them he can almost vicariously achieve his goals, dreams and ambitions.

Karmically this individual may himself be an escapist but it would trouble him if he allowed his friends or the world to take the same path. He himself escapes to transform and can be of great personal help to others by his not being personally bound to the world.

RETROGRADE PLUTO
IN THE TWELFTH HOUSE

With this placement the individual nearly always experiences Phase III of the Retrograde Process. He is highly introspective and unusually deep in his awareness of life as it is. He feels the bindings of society in his inner mind, but has the power to break free from them if he chooses.

Often he is highly secretive, for he himself is not fully in touch with the depth of his motives. Still he sees enough to know that much of his outer life is forced by society and makes him a hypocrite to his inner being. Great periods of loneliness and despondence are experienced. The person feels misunderstood. He often would like to see tiresome situations brought to an end and as a result of this he can consciously stimulate destructive forces in those around him. Of all in the Zodiac this individual can be the most negative in respect to the positive efforts of others to help pull him out of his shell.The use of drugs is dangerous to this person, as they only tend to remove him further from a state of presence in the reality of the here and now. Karmically he is trying to find meaning in his Soul and through a very hectic process of elimination he will eventually discard all that has no meaning to him so that he can ultimately identify with his essence. His journey is into the unknown regions of Man and his Universe, and while he may experience the greatest of difficulties along the way, his reward will be the finding of his Soul.